YO-BVN-835

JCSS Study No. 2

ASALA — IRRATIONAL TERROR OR POLITICAL TOOL

Anat Kurz and Ariel Merari

A15012 056781

HV
6433
.T9
K87x
1985
WEST

ASU WEST LIBRARY

ISBN 0-8133-0324-9 (Westview)
LC 85-51350 (Westview)

JCSS Studies
are published for the Jaffee Center
for Strategic Studies
by
The Jerusalem Post
POB 81, Jerusalem 91000, Israel
and
Westview Press
Boulder, Colorado 80301, Frederick A. Praeger, Publisher

Printed in Israel at the Jerusalem Post Press

Copyright © 1985
Tel Aviv University
Jaffee Center for Strategic Studies

All rights reserved. No part of this book may be reproduced in any
form or by any electronic or mechanical means without permission
in writing from Tel Aviv University.

Table of Contents

Summary

The Armenian terrorist organization ASALA began its activities in January 1975 in Beirut, and since then has secured itself a place within the international terrorist system. During the past decade dozens of Turkish diplomats have been attacked by Armenian terrorists, and even western states have been the target of terrorist campaigns.

The roots of Armenian terror must be sought in an accumulation of frustration resulting from the international community's lack of interest in the Armenian tragedy, and a general tendency to ignore or deny the slaughter of this nation perpetrated in Turkey in the course of World War I. During the mid-1970s the militant revolutionary atmosphere surrounding the civil war in Lebanon inspired and stimulated young Armenians to take recourse to the ultimate protest — political terrorism. The ideology informing ASALA's activities is therefore nationalistic and leftist, with a strong accent on motives such as revenge on Turkey, and on forcing the world to recognize the historic injustice inflicted on the Armenians. In addition, ASALA aims at the liberation of the Armenian territories in Turkey, and their unification with the Soviet Armenian areas. One of the intermediate goals of the organization is to turn the movement into a popular or mass struggle, but at the present moment this objective seems rather ambitious, as the organization counts only several dozen members.

With the exception of several incidents of a more demonstrative nature, ASALA's activities have concentrated mainly on assassinations and bomb attacks, primarily in the Middle East and Europe. In the absence of a territorial infrastructure and the means to exert political pressure, the organization depends for its continued existence on the support of larger bodies. It was established with the aid of Palestinian groups in Lebanon, and it is they who, over the years, have provided the main assistance in terms of weapons and training facilities. This support base was seriously impaired during the Lebanon War in the summer of 1982, and since then ASALA has been faced with critical logistics difficulties. This has resulted in ideological conflicts, which in turn have caused a split within the organization: several factions which broke away following the terrorist evacuation of Beirut have moved to Syrian-dominated areas in eastern Lebanon and to Iran, and this raises questions as to the organization's freedom of action now and in the future. Another faction, less extreme as regards modus operandi, has turned toward Europe, in particular Greece, Cyprus and France, but it appears to lack the human and logistics infrastructure required to maintain activities on the level of previous years.

Since 1980 ASALA has posed a problem for the European states, Canada and the United States, in whose territories it has been active. The arrest of Armenian terrorists on their soil was answered in the majority of cases by a wave of reprisals; terrorism, as a means of pressuring these countries (mainly France and Switzerland) to release jailed members, formed the organization's principal activity. In the summer of 1983, following an explosion at Orly Airport, the French government decided to take a much firmer stand against the Armenian terrorists, and since then ASALA has ceased to operate on its territory. In other fields of operation, i.e., the Middle East, only isolated activities have been registered. In addition to the customary and systematic pursuit of Turkish diplomats, these have been aimed at French targets.

Within the international community, ASALA has made a major contribution to creating an awareness of the Armenian tragedy. The organization may also be credited with the nationalist awakening among Armenian youth in the world at large: an Armenian terror organization, the JCAG, was even established in the United States.

ASALA's political aim — the national liberation of historic Armenia — would seem irrational today. Even so, its declared strategy constitutes an ideological framework for those who see struggle per se as a preferred, if not the sole, means of expression. Difficulties which have manifested themselves during the past two years have brought about a considerable decrease in the frequency of attacks. But, considering the motives underlying its activities, it must be assumed that the threat which ASALA poses in Turkey and other countries has not diminished.

I. Introduction

In 1973 two Turkish diplomats were shot in Los Angeles by an 80-year old Armenian named Kirkan Yanikian. Behind this act of revenge by a lone individual lay a national reawakening among the dispersed Armenians in the world, which had begun in the early 1970s. This incident might gradually have been forgotten, had it not in fact catalyzed a chain of events which turned it, and its perpetrator, into a symbol signifying the end of the conspiracy of silence which since 1915 had surrounded the holocaust of the Armenian people. Since 1975 some 30 Turkish diplomats or members of their families have been attacked in dozens of terrorist actions, with the result that Armenian revenge, as well as the background to the Armenian struggle, have become a near permanent feature in the world press. These terrorist acts were actually carried out by a small group of people, but due to their spectacular nature they were successful in bringing the Armenian tragedy to the forefront of international awareness.

The resort to terrorism emerged among the international Armenian community 50 years after the Armenians had become a nation of refugees. The events in eastern Anatolia during World War I, and the large-scale expulsion of the Armenians from their soil, in the course of which over half the Armenian population of Turkey was massacred, became the bedrock of the collective memory of this nation. As time passed, a feeling of deep frustration developed over the lack of public interest in what eventually would be recognized as the first genocide in the 20th century. During previous decades Armenian political bodies kept up a steady stream of restrained and generally unproductive activity, aimed at focusing attention on the subject and achieving official recognition of the historical suffering caused to the Armenians. But during the past fifteen years a change in climate has occurred. In the early 1970s a national reawakening became noticeable among the dispersed Armenians in the world, which must in part be ascribed to the realization that the political road had been a failure. The extreme expression of this tendency was the recourse of young Armenians to violent struggle.

Armenian terror has two central objectives: the first — as expressed in the activities of the JCAG (Justice Commando for the Armenian Genocide) is informed mainly by a desire for revenge against Turkey and its legations worldwide. The larger, and more intimidating Armenian organization is ASALA (Armenian Secret Army for the Liberation of Armenia), which forms the subject of this study.

Beyond a desire for revenge, ASALA is fighting for national liberation, and its ultimate aim is the restoration of historical Armenia to the Armenian nation. ASALA is distinguished from other organizations with a separatist signature, in that it does not fight an alien regime inside its homeland, but from outside its borders. There are today some five million Armenians in the world, approximately four million of whom reside in the Soviet Union, but in Turkish Armenia hardly any Armenians are left. The Soviet Union, which controls the largest part of Armenia, does not form a target for Armenian terror: according to ASALA's conception Soviet Armenia is liberated, and one of the organization's aims is to turn it into a territory from which the national Armenian struggle can be conducted.

The absence of a popular support base within its homeland constitutes a critical limitation for any organization with nationalist aspirations. In the present case this has dictated the central characteristics of ASALA, and in effect has determined the nature of the international framework within which the organization operates. Its activists hail from Armenian population concentrations in the Middle East, Europe and the North American continent. These parts of the world, particularly Europe, are also the locales where terrorist attacks are carried out. Thus, even though Turkey forms the main objective of the attacks, ASALA activity, a priori, always indirectly involves at least one other state. An operational scope of this nature is virtually unparalleled: the arena of the struggle in fact encompasses any location where there are either Turkish legations, or legations of western nations that have provoked ASALA's enmity by fighting the Armenian terror conducted on their territory.

Apart from this, ASALA considers its struggle an inseparable part of the national liberation struggles of oppressed peoples. This ideological identification would not satisfy the need ASALA has felt from the day of its foundation for the backing of stronger and more established bodies than itself, were not this support also expressed in a more tangible form. ASALA was in fact established under the protection of the PLO in Lebanon; it was from the Palestinian nationalist movement that it drew its inspiration, and Palestinian terror served as a model for the type of struggle it chose to conduct. This support base was seriously impaired in the course of the Lebanon War during the summer of 1982, forcing ASALA to search for a new framework. In this particular case it did not have to look far: today the organization's principal bases remain in Lebanon, but in the areas under Syrian control. Thus, while the struggle was fundamentally born out of a sense of distress, as well as nationalist motives, internationalist motivations also play a role in ASALA's activity, and it has formed, from the moment of its inception, a part of a wider terrorist system.

The constraints affecting ASALA's activity raise serious questions as to the fundamental rationality of its struggle: can its activities in the international sphere, as they are conducted today, form a step on the way to real political achievements? What are the prospects for bridging ideological gaps and geographical dispersion within the internal Armenian context? What are the possibilities for influencing global political frameworks indirectly related to the Armenian case, in such a way as to bring ASALA closer to the realization of the national aspirations it represents?

ASALA's activities have found a response among the Armenian communities in the world. The organization's appearance has led to a polarization of attitudes at both sides of the spectrum, as well as the creation of new currents, both political and terrorist (e.g., JCAG), among the exiles. Despite unequivocal denunciations of violent struggle, ASALA's acts of violence have undeniably revived the Armenian problem in the eyes of the world. This development would not have taken place had ASALA not taken the terrorist direction — however limited in scope — and herein lies its main, and most striking achievement.

The ASALA phenomenon is of special interest to the Jewish people and to Israel for several reasons. Both Jews and Armenians have been the victims of genocide in the 20th century. The establishment of ASALA was a belated reaction to the holocaust which struck the Armenian people, and an indirect result of the conversion of Beirut into the terrorist capital of the world during the 1970s.

ASALA's incorporation into the Middle Eastern terrorist complex, the fact that it was assisted from the outset by the Palestinian terror organizations, as well as its present connections with Syria, combine to make Israel a potential target for the organization's terrorist activity. Even so, to date ASALA has carried out no direct operations against Israeli targets. A possible explanation involves two principal considerations. The first concerns the limited scope of the Armenian-Israeli context, and the parallels between Armenian history and that of the Jews, which far outweigh differences in the political sphere. Secondly, present-day Israel provides an example of national rehabilitation (even though the conditions under which this was brought about cannot be separated from their specific time-frame), and thus has earned for Israel and the Zionist movement the sympathy of the Armenian people. In the wider context, our efforts to understand why ASALA has not acted against Israel cannot be divorced from the fact that, notwithstanding the intensive terrorist activity conducted by the organization against western nations, it has not digressed from activities that are related to the Armenian cause. It therefore appears that ASALA will not attack Israeli targets as long as Israel, for its part, refrains from moving directly against it, thereby ranging itself on the side of the enemies of the Armenian nationalist movement.

II. Historical Background

The Armenian Holocaust

Armenia — a country linking Central Asia to Turkish Anatolia — has throughout the course of its history been a regional bone of contention in which alternating regimes have held sway. During the middle of the 15th century the country, together with the Kurdish, Turkish and Armenian principalities on its territory, became part of the Ottoman Empire. At the beginning of the 19th century, when the power of the Empire was already declining, Russia and the western powers began to encroach upon its independence, by establishing their individual spheres of influence in the area.

These developments accentuate the critical conjunction of specific circumstances — an ethnic, religious and national minority occupying a strategically important border area — which in effect brought about the tragic fate of the Armenians. The Armenians have lived in eastern Anatolia since the dawn of history, but except for a period of some three centuries, from the 8th century AD onwards, the only independent Armenian state existed for a short period at the beginning of the 20th century.

Christianity was declared the national religion in the 3rd century AD even before it became the official religion of the Roman Empire, and throughout the generations the Armenians preserved their religious distinctiveness and national identity, never intermixing with their Muslim neighbors. Until the beginning of the 19th century the Armenian nation constituted a majority in its areas of residence, but when Russian penetration heightened Ottoman sensitivities with regard to the eastern provinces of the Empire, Kurds and Turks were also settled in Armenia. At the same time a change occurred in the tolerant atmosphere toward minorities that had prevailed in the Empire during previous centuries; they began to be considered a threatening and potentially dissident factor. But unlike others — Serbians, Bulgarians, Greeks — the Armenians were by this time a minority in their own habitat, and this made them an easy target for persecution. In 1928 the Russians occupied several parts of Armenia, including the area of Edjimiatzin (the residence of the Catholicos, the primate of the Armenian Church). The authorities now began to incite the Kurds against the Armenians residing in the border regions, and any efforts at nationalist expression on the part of the latter were suppressed.

These tendencies caused repercussions in Europe, and in 1863, under pressure from the Powers — France and Great Britain — Armenia was declared a separate nation within the framework of the Ottoman Empire. But this step, too, failed to create a real change in its position. The justification for European and Russian efforts to intervene in the internal policies of the Empire was the protection of Christian interests in the Muslim world, but all efforts to carry through reforms only caused increasing hostility on the part of the Muslims — against minorities in general, and the Armenians in particular.

Meanwhile, a nationalist sensitivity was developing among the Armenians. In 1853 a group of Armenian intellectuals met in Paris to promote the severing of Armenia from the nations — Persia, Russia, and Turkey — which ruled parts of its historic territory. These aspirations were backed by France, but the principal support came from the side of Russia. Cooperation between Armenian separatist elements and Russia increased following the signing of the Treaty of San Stefano in 1878, which forced the Ottoman sultan to acquiesce in Russian protection of Christians throughout the Empire. At the same time Great Britain undertook to guarantee implementation of the conditions of the agreement, while the Russians received the Kars, Batoum, and Ardahan areas in eastern Anatolia. This border region, with its predominantly Armenian population, remained a bone of contention between Russia and the Ottoman Empire for some hundred years, from 1828 until the end of World War I.

In this atmosphere of increasing friction between the Armenian population and the Ottoman authorities, and under the impact of the nationalist reawakening which swept through Europe at the end of the 19th century, the years 1885-1890 saw the founding of the first Armenian political parties: the Armanakan Party flourished among the Armenian population of the Van region in Turkey, the socialist-oriented Hunchak ("bell") Party was founded by Armenian students in Geneva, and the nationalist Dashnak, or Dashnakisutiun (Revolutionary Armenian Federation) Party was founded in Tiflis (Tbilisi) in Georgia — though more as a reaction to the persecutions of the Tsar than to those of the Ottoman regime.[1]

These first nationalist stirrings intensified a Turkish sense of the potential threat posed by Armenian concentrations in the eastern part of the Empire. Pogroms during the years 1895-96 resulted in the death of thousands of Armenians in Istanbul and the eastern provinces.[2] Their immediate cause was the occupation of a bank in Istanbul by a group of Armenians. Predictably, these incidents reinforced the nationalistic tendencies among the Armenians, in particular within the ranks of the Dashnaks. Still, the party did not call for any changes beyond political reform and cultural autonomy within a federal framework, either in Russia or in Turkey. Certainly no clearcut demands for independence were voiced.

In 1908 the Young Turks movement, which belonged to the Ittihad — the Revolutionary Committee of Union and Progress — was co-opted into the Turkish government within a new parliamentary framework. This party, too, was nurtured by the prevailing European nationalist atmosphere, and advocated the unification of all the inhabitants of the Empire, regardless of their national or religious affiliation. The Armenian Dashnak Party supported the new group, and as a gesture of goodwill, no less than in the expectation of reforms, called a halt to Armenian guerrilla activities in the eastern regions which it had instigated intermittently since 1895. But Armenian hopes were to be disappointed: cooperation remained largely an empty letter, and revolutionary protests against lack of equality failed to strike a chord among the Muslim population of Turkey, while revolutionary reforms in the government system failed to obtain the support of Sultan Abdulhamid himself. In April 1909 the sultan instigated a counter-coup to eliminate the Young Turks; the latter not only stood their ground, but even turned on the Armenians, accusing them of collaborating with the sultan. During disturbances that year in the Adana region of Cilicia more than 30,000 Armenians were massacred. During the following years, until the outbreak of World War I in 1914, the Young Turks turned their efforts toward consolidation of their regime: the prevailing nationalistic atmosphere formed the basis of a pan-Turkish ideology, in addition to stirring up ambitions to renew the days of the Empire's dominance in Asia.

This atmosphere affected the Muslim minorities outside the borders of the Empire: those living on Russian territory expected Turkish support, while the Christian inhabitants of the Ottoman Empire turned for protection to the Tsar (Muslim nationalism in Russia was awakened during the early years of the 20th century, and as early as 1905 clashes occurred between Armenian and Muslim nationalists in Baku in Russia).[3]

On the eve of World War I the Armenians had come to a point where their continually worsening situation was in fact determined by outside forces which they themselves were in no position to control. Further deterioration was caused by inflammatory speeches that raised the specter of disloyalty in all the states where they were residing — Russia, Turkey, and Persia. Pogroms and repressive measures increased Armenian nationalist and separatist tendencies, resulting in turn in an intensification of repressive measures by the authorities. Reports on the treatment to which the Armenians were subjected under the Ottoman regime, especially after the middle of the 19th century, reached Europe — but efforts at intervention on the part of the western states, and western demands for political reform (prompted by strategic interest as well as sincere feelings) only contributed to the local conception of the Armenian people as a destabilizing factor within the imperial framework.

On November 2, 1914, Turkey declared *Jihad* and joined the world war on the side of Germany and the Austro-Hungarian Empire. Although the Armenian political groups which had been members of the government since 1908 had supported Turkish neutrality in the war, they nevertheless now called on Armenian youth to fulfill their duties as Ottoman citizens. But upon the outbreak of hostilities, the Dashnak Party refused to accede to the government's demand to instigate an Armenian uprising in Russian Transcaucasia. This refusal, coupled with accusations of Armenian activities on behalf of Russia (at around the same time Armenians in Transcaucasia were publicly advocating the liberation of Turkish Armenia), prepared the ground for the events that would from then on be known as "the 1915 massacre."

Immediately following the outbreak of hostilities, the Russians invaded Turkish Armenia, and by the winter of 1915 three out of the seven Armenian provinces — Bitlis, Van, and Erzerum — formed the center of the combat area. On May 30, 1915 the Ottoman minister of the interior, Talaat Pasha, signed an order for the mass transfer of the Armenian population from its areas of residence in eastern Turkey toward Iraq and the Syrian desert. The official pretext for this step was the removal of Armenians from sensitive areas, to prevent any possibility of their harming the internal security of the state. This reasoning lacked any practical basis, for

although Armenian political groups had refused active cooperation with the government against Russia, and despite the defection
of Armenian elements to the Russian side, the Armenian population as a whole did not turn against the government.

On April 24, 1915, several days before the issue of the official
order, 650 Armenian leaders were arrested in Istanbul, thus
rendering the Armenian nation leaderless at the very moment the
expulsions began. The first stage was the evacuation of the
Armenian settlements in the eastern districts. The inhabitants
were given one or two days to prepare themselves, and before the
convoys set out the men were separated from the women and
children. Numerous evacuees were shot at only a short distance
from their villages, and the ranks of those who continued were
thinned as a result of their passage through combat areas,
ambushes by soldiers and civilians en route, and starvation.[4]

Simultaneously officers and soldiers of Armenian origin were
removed from the army, thus effectively preventing the establishment of a protective force to shield the exiles. In the second stage,
the army turned on the Armenian population in central Turkey,
Anatolia, and Cilicia. The general destination of the convoys was
Aleppo in Syria, and here about 400,000 to 500,000 deportees
passed before being shunted on to the Syrian desert or Iraq.
Subsequent claims have it that about 60% of the entire Armenian
population of Turkey, or 1,500,000 persons, were either massacred
or died during the march. According to other, lower estimates of
the number of victims, 1.2 million persons died out of a population
of 1.7 million Armenians living in Turkey on the eve of the war.[5]
Still lower estimates speak of 600,000-700,000 victims.[6]

In the absence of historical documentation, the real number of
victims remains an open question, although the facts of the
genocide as such (except for the official Turkish position to date)
are nowhere disputed. During the months in which the expulsions
took place, reports reached the West from missionaries, teachers
of Christian schools, Red Cross officials and western diplomats.
They addressed emotional appeals to their governments; Henry
Morgenthau, the American ambassador in Turkey, even conducted
direct negotiations with Ottoman Interior Minister Talaat Pasha,
and Minister of War Enver Pasha. These testimonies include
photographs of the convoys and written memoirs, and bear
witness to the fact that we are not dealing here merely with a
collective population transfer, which (as the Turkish government

claimed) caused a "reasonable" number of victims, but with systematic genocide.

Apart from this, efforts at determining the precise number of casualties lose significance in light of the simple fact that by the end of World War I almost no Armenians were left in the eastern provinces of Turkey. Some 300,000 Armenians who had fled to Russia, or found themselves in areas occupied by the latter, were saved, as were another 100,000 who resided in the large cities of central and western Turkey, where the authorities found it more difficult to resort to the extreme measures they had taken in the remote areas of the country.

Immediately after the close of World War I, Turkish policy toward the Armenian question was in effect dictated by the victorious European nations. On July 5, 1919, with Turkey now under the revolutionary regime of Mustapha Kemal, the trial opened in Istanbul of the leaders of the Young Turks movement under whom Turkey had conducted the war. Called the Trial of the Unionists, it pronounced severe sentences against those found responsible for the planning and execution of the massacre of the Armenian nation. (Subsequently, a systematic Turkish effort would be made to obfuscate the striking significance of the indictments in this trial).

Talaat Pasha, who had signed the expulsion orders, Enver Pasha, and Jemal Pasha, who had served as minister of the navy, were sentenced to death in absentia (they had fled from Turkey to Europe). Most high government officials of the Young Turks' regime were similarly tried and sentenced to extended prison terms.[7]

In 1918 Transcaucasia declared its independence, and a regional federation was established — but after only a few months this split up into three separate republics: Georgia, Azerbaijan and Armenia. Turkey, while officially recognizing the independence of the republics, simultaneously took military steps to retrieve some of the territories in the Kars, Ardahan and Batoum regions. These, at the time, formed a part of the Armenian republic, but under the terms of the Treaty of Brest-Litovsk, signed at the beginning of 1918 between Bolshevik Russia and Turkey, they were to have come under Turkish rule. Fighting in these regions between Turkish forces and the Armenians continued until 1920, parallel to the political processes that had been initiated following the end of the war. The latter were concluded only in 1923, at which time the definitive borders and the division of spheres of influence among the regional powers were finally agreed. On December 2, 1920, the Armenian Republic collapsed under the weight of external and domestic pressures. That day the Armenian government at Yerevan gave up the Kars and Ardahan regions to the Turks, while Bolsheviks seized Yerevan and turned the rest of Armenia into a part of the Soviet Union.

Armenian representatives were a partner to the international discussions held following the end of the war, including the Conference of Sèvres. But the Treaty of Sèvres that was signed on August 10, 1920, which granted international recognition to Armenian independence, was devoid of any practical significance. Earlier, during the Conference of San Remo, which had taken place in April of the same year as part of the peace settlement between Turkey and the United States, the latter had been assigned the responsibility of defining the Armenian borders. The Armenians, for their part, did not agree to an American mandate over their territory, while the League of Nations refused to admit Armenia as a member nation on the grounds that — as a part of the Soviet Union — it was not an independent state.

In March 1921, after Yerevan had been encircled by the Red Army, the Turkish Kemalists and the Soviets signed the Treaty of Moscow, which satisfied the demands of the territorialists on both sides. Armenia, a region which according to the delineation made by the United States comprised an area of 72,000 km^2, was divided between the two countries. The eastern region, comprising some 30,000 km^2 which since December 2, 1920 had de facto formed a part of the Soviet Union, was formally annexed by the latter.

The brief interlude of Armenian independence had come to an end. On July 23, 1923 Kemalist Turkey and the western Powers signed the Treaty of Lausanne, which recognized the Turkish boundaries — with not a single mention being made of Armenia.[8]

The events of World War I turned the Armenian people into a nation of refugees. But the large waves of emigration during these years were only a continuation of earlier waves in Armenia's long history, during which they had established settlements outside their own country.

The first Armenian settlement in Russia dated from as early as the 12th century, when Armenia passed under Kurdish sovereignty. At that time Armenians fled to Georgia, the Crimea and elsewhere. In 1605 the Persian Shah Abbas displaced thousands of

Armenians, relocating them next to his capital Isafahan. They formed the foundation of the large Armenian community in Persia which, like the communities on Russian territory, was not harmed during the war. The beginning of the 19th century, following the Russian penetration into Armenia, saw the resumption of immigration to the Transcaucasian region. And following the pogroms of 1895-96. large groups of Armenians emigrated to countries as far away as India and Indonesia.

After the war, in 1919, some 80,000 Armenian survivors returned from Syria to their previous domiciles where, in many places — principally in Cilicia — they were once more subjected to attacks from the Kemalist military forces. When in September 1921 France resigned its mandate over the region, 50,000-60,000 Armenians returned to Syria and Lebanon which remained mandated to France.[9]

In 1922 Soviet Armenia was merged with Azerbaijan and Georgia, forming the Transcaucasian Soviet Federation, but it reverted to an autonomous republic when the federation was dissolved in 1936. In 1945 the Soviet Union issued a call to the Armenians to return to Armenia within the framework of a repatriation campaign. The appeal was answered by close to 100,000 persons — the majority of whom came from the Middle East.[10]

The Armenian Diaspora Today

There is a certain lack of coherence in quantitative data about the present-day Armenian diaspora. Estimates speak of approximately five million persons, of whom some four million are in the Soviet Union. Three million of these constitute approximately 90% of the total population of the Yerevan district of Soviet Armenia. Others reside in Azerbaijan, Russia, Karbah, and Georgia. There are additional Armenian concentrations in the West, originating with the waves of emigration from the Middle East, particularly — in the Americas — in the United States (approx. 500,000) and Canada (approx. 100,000), in addition to smaller communities in Argentina and Brazil. There are today some 300,000 Armenians in Europe, approximately a quarter million of whom live in France. About 500,000 Armenians live in the Middle East, including approximately 200,000 in Iran, 100,000 in Lebanon, and some

100,000 in Syria. Smaller concentrations can be found in Ethiopia, South Africa, and Australia.[11]

In Turkey there are today approximately 50,000-60,000 Armenians (some sources state their number at 80,000 persons),[12] the majority of whom live in Istanbul, Ankara, and Van. In the Turkish areas of Armenia there are today hardly any Armenians left, the region mainly being populated by Kurds.

Historically, the Armenian protest movement is related primarily not to the demand for the liberation of the historical homeland, but rather to the ongoing quest for international recognition of the mass murders and historic injustice caused to the nation.

In 1920 the Dashnak Party founded a revenge network called "Nemesis" whose objective was to strike at Ottoman officials considered responsible for the slaughter. Talaat Pasha was shot on March 15, 1921 in Berlin. His assailant, a young Armenian called Sochoman Tehlirian, surrendered to the police immediately following the act, but in the subsequent trial was acquitted by virtue of the historical accusations leveled against his victim and the regime he represented. Three other Ottoman leaders were attacked by the same group: the former foreign minister, Said Halim, was shot in Rome, and two other officials were shot in Berlin. The trial of Tehlirian, and the subsequent developments connected with the event, aroused worldwide public attention. But from then on, for nearly another 50 years, interest in the "Armenian cause" died away. On April 24, 1965 the 50th anniversary of the slaughter was commemorated with unofficial demonstrations in Yerevan in Soviet Armenia, but apart from a review in the French press these failed to raise echoes anywhere in the world. Neither did the Armenian diaspora itself voice any meaningful political demands over the years for recognition of national rights.

The turning point came around the middle of the 1970s, when the Armenian issue once more hit the headlines. This development resulted from both a change in climate among the Armenian communities in the West, and the fact that certain groups among them began to take recourse to a new and violent mode of expression.

The Emergence of the Armenian Terrorist Movements

The year 1975 saw the rise of two Armenian terrorist movements, ASALA and JCAG-1. Together they introduced a new era in the Armenian nationalist struggle.

Three factors combined to create this development:

1. The succession of disappointments within the Armenian community with the lack of results from political action;
2. the flourishing of international terror as a political weapon;
3. the inspiration provided by the Palestinian nationalist movement and its armed struggle.

In 1974 a United Nations committee on the rights of man was appointed; in its report, it completely failed to mention the genocide of the Armenian people.[13] Although creating bitter disappointment among Armenian bodies, which had consistently limited themselves to diplomatic activity alone, this fact in itself hardly warranted recourse to violent struggle. It did, however, cause defections among the younger members of the main, old-established Armenian political parties, the Dashnak and Hunshak, with their basically nationalist signature. The defections represented the continuation of a trend which had already emerged within the Armenian community during the early 1960s, when the first protest calls were sounded against the restrained way in which the traditional leadership groups among the exiles had conducted the political struggle up to that time. Thus the foundation was laid for the creation of an independent militant body.

These currents were influenced by the rising wave of international political terrorism in Europe and the Middle East since the end of the 1960s, and particularly at the beginning of the 1970s. The significance of this phenomenon lay mainly in the way ideological radicalism was being diverted to new channels. It was accompanied by a climate of identification with, and tolerance of, national liberation struggles in the world at large.

Parallel with this, young Armenians in Lebanon were exposed to the Palestinian nationalist struggle and its attendant leftist ideology. In effect, from the outset ASALA was supported by the PLO in Beirut. Intensive ideological and logistics connections were established between the organizations, in particular between

ASALA and the PFLP — the Popular Front for the Liberation of Palestine — which had a Marxist ideological basis.

The founding of ASALA in January 1975, and the alternative operational methods it proposed, created a conceptual division within the Armenian population of Beirut. Intensification of the ties between the Armenian and Palestinian factions in Beirut was accompanied by a sizable migration of Armenians from the eastern suburbs of Beirut, where they had for decades lived among the Christian population, to the Muslim western suburbs — the stronghold of the Palestinians. All this took place against the backdrop of the Lebanese civil war.[14]

Increasing Armenian popular support for ASALA resulted in a decision that same year by the traditional rightist party, the Dashnak, to establish an organization of its own — the JCAG. Its first action was the assassination of the Turkish ambassador in Vienna on October 22, 1975.

Since then, the scope of ASALA's actions has broadened to a point where at present attacks on western, non-Turkish targets constitute the majority of its activities. But the JCAG has remained faithful to its original objective, in the sense that it restricts itself to attacks on Turkish targets. This organization operates mainly in the United States, but has also carried out operations in Europe — and even behind the Iron Curtain.

Another Armenian organization, which emerged for the first time in 1977, is the NAR, the New Armenian Resistance. It has claimed responsibility for seven attacks, three of which were also claimed by ASALA. Opinions are divided as to the background and identity of this organization. According to some, the NAR is an offshoot of an even more nationalistic Armenian ideological current than that which gave rise to the JCAG. According to another version, the NAR is employed by ASALA — which embraces a leftist ideology — to strike in particular at Soviet targets (although not all NAR attacks were directed against legations of the Soviet Union). Since 1980 the organization has not carried out a single attack.

From the year of its foundation, and in particular since 1979, there has been a steady increase in the frequency of ASALA's activities. This has been accompanied by a broadening of its geographical range of action, beyond the Middle East to Europe and North America, even including a shift to attacks on European targets as a means of pressuring countries which have arrested members of the organization.

The Lebanon War and the evacuation of the PLO from Beirut in September 1982 forced ASALA to abandon its bases, which since its foundation had been located in Beirut, and to look for new logistics bases, and even new patrons. This reality brought to the surface several conceptional and tactical struggles within ASALA, which may have existed before the need for reorganization arose. These evidently caused divisions, and even led to the secession of parts of the organization. But in light of trends which characterized ASALA's activities prior to September 1982, and even following the evacuation of Beirut, the threat it poses to Turkey, as well as to the western nations, would appear not to have diminished.

III. Asala's Terrorist Activities

The Ideological and Strategic Platform

ASALA's terrorist activities are dictated first and foremost by a desire for revenge on Turkey; attacks on Turkish legations throughout the world are the primary means by which the struggle is conducted.

In addition, the organization aims at forcing the international community to recognize the historic injustice inflicted upon the Armenian nation. And it sees the struggle as an instrument for the national reunification of a dispersed people. In the words of Abu Mujahed, believed to be the code name of the leader of ASALA, Hagop Hagopian, during an interview in Lebanon in August 1983:

> Primary objectives are to introduce the Armenian cause to world public opinion, and make the world feel that there is a desolate people that lacks homeland or identity, and to arouse the national feeling of the Armenian diaspora.[15]

On several occasions, spokesmen for the organization have deviated from this demand for recognition of an historic injustice by including an actual political claim — the right of the Armenian people to return to its historic homeland in Armenia. Thus, according to Mihran Mihranian (another code name of Hagop Hagopian) in an interview quoted in March 1983:

> We demand the clear and unequivocal recognition of the massacres, and of our right to settle on our own soil, and there to establish our own nation. We are prepared for the revolutionary burden this imposes upon us, however bloody the price that we might have to pay. The important thing for us is that people are with us and have placed their trust in us.[16]

ASALA's ultimate declared goal is the liberation from Turkey of the Armenian regions bordering on Iran, Iraq and Syria, and their unification with the Armenian territory which forms a part of the Soviet Union, which is considered liberated.[17] In this connection, the call for the unification of Armenia within the framework of the Soviet Union might be seen as a more realistic possibility than the unification of the Armenian territories within a completely independent framework.

ASALA considers itself a part of the international revolutionary movement. As such it belongs to a long list of organizations — such as the Basque ETA, the IRA, and certain Palestinian groups —

whose nationalist struggle is characterized by a leftist ideological stamp.

> Let Imperialism and its collaborators all over the world know that their institutions are targets for our heros and will be destroyed. We will kill and destroy because that is the only language understood by Imperialism.[18]

On at least one occasion this ideological theme found expression in a more comprehensive ideological context. In October 1983 the Cypriot newspaper *Al Nashara* published a wide-ranging article about ASALA, which was remarkable for the amount of detail it provided, as well as its emphasis on the long-range political aims of the impending struggle. According to the ASALA spokesman who gave the interview, the organization's political platform embraces the following points:

1. ASALA is a political organization whose purpose is to mobilize the Armenian people for the struggle to liberate the Armenian territories from the colonialist oppression of the Turks and their imperialist and international reactionary henchmen, by every means of struggle.
2. The Army (i.e., ASALA) is guided by the theory of world revolution.
3. The Army represents the ambitions of the Armenian people in its opposition to the national and class servitude imposed upon it by the ruling clique in Turkey.
4. The Army believes in revolutionary terrorist activity as a fundamental principle, and as the proper weapon for fighting exploitation and oppression, and eliminating Turkish colonialism — even though the organization does not rule out other methods of conducting its struggle.
5. The Army forms a part of the world-revolutionary movement, for which reason it makes every effort to strengthen its ties with the revolutionary movement, in the belief that world-wide unity of all revolutionaries is one of the requirements for overcoming the problem of the oppressed and persecuted peoples and classes.
6. The liberation of the Armenian territories from Turkish domination will result in their unification with the adjoining parts of Armenia and the establishment of a single democratic revolutionary organization.
7. The Army will conduct its struggle everywhere in the

world where the Armenian people live and where the Turkish enemy maintains its interests and legations.

8. [It aims at] convincing the Soviet Union and other socialist countries to support the Armenian cause and assist the Armenian people in Soviet Armenia, in order to create a revolutionary spearhead for a long-term people's war, aimed at the destruction of Turkish colonialism.[19]

The conditions required for realization of these objectives, as voiced by the ASALA spokesman, correspond with the objectives the organization has adopted for itself, as well as with its declared ideological line (although the language of the article implies that these objectives have so far not been achieved):

1. The establishment of a people's army.
2. The establishment of a popular front, embracing representatives of all revolutionary strata and opponents of imperialism and colonialism, and opposing all kinds of persecution and oppression.
3. The establishment of a revolutionary political party to lead and direct the people's army and the national front.[20]

This strategic framework indicates that ASALA's objectives differ from mere revenge on Turkey. During the first years of its activities the organization, with one exception, attacked Turkish legations only. (The first strike it carried out, in January 1975, was directed against the headquarters of the World Council of Churches in Beirut. This institution was chosen because of activities which, according to ASALA, were intended to encourage the emigration of Armenians to the United States.[21])

In 1979 ASALA began to attack western targets, a shift defined as the "second stage" of its activity:

Our second step was only possible due to the successful completion of our first step which had politicized the Armenian youth enough to gain their support in the second step. The second step contains four new developments:

1. Heavy assault on imperialist, Zionist and reactionary forces;
2. a much greater frequency of attacks;
3. direct communication with the Armenian masses and international opinion; and
4. strong ties with other organizations....[22]

The international revolutionary motif is clearly expressed in

ASALA's strategic platform as quoted above, even though, judging by its operations in the course of the years, it does not constitute a central and leading element. Indeed, the organization at present does not appear actually to adhere to its declared strategic theme: in 1979 a tendency became noticeable for ASALA to distance itself from its initial objectives, namely attacks against Turkey and bringing the Armenian question to the attention of the world, even though a review of the organization's activities from 1980 onwards shows that this change did not mean the abandonment of the previous operational framework. Thus, even if from 1980 onward attacks on western targets have formed ASALA's primary activity, this must be considered a result of direct "provocations" against ASALA or the Armenian people, rather than as a concerted drive against "imperialism." This discrepancy between the organization's official political platform and the nature of its actual struggle emerges again and again in reviews of the stages of ASALA's activities undertaken through the years.

The periods in the life of ASALA are not clearly defined. Some operational trends, motifs and aims of an individual period continue to be evidenced during part of the succeeding period, such as the steadily increasing frequency of operations, and a mounting escalation in the selection of targets. To this must be added a number of external factors which have left their mark on the organization, such as the Lebanon War, and the evacuation of Beirut in the summer of 1982. Even so, three main periods in the life of ASALA can be distinguished: during the years 1975-79 the organization concentrated its attacks on Turkish targets; from 1979 onward the choice of objectives broadened to include attacks on western targets — mainly as reprisal against countries that had acted against ASALA; and the period from 1982 until the present day has witnessed continuation of the policy of attacks against western nations which have arrested ASALA members, as well as a tendency toward attacks of a more demonstrative nature. This same period has revealed conflicts within the organization, and a rift has occurred. The above periods may be considered as landmarks with regard to ASALA's evolution in terms of the frequency of its activities, its choice of targets, and areas of operation. On the basis of cumulative data and testimonies, we shall attempt to evaluate the deviations from ASALA's declared political platform, as well as the processes which have brought ASALA to its present position.

The Early Years: 1975 – 1979

During the first years ASALA carried out few actions, and limited its choice of targets. Only three to four attacks were carried out annually and these were directed against Turkish legations and individuals. Most of these attacks took place in Beirut, but attacks on Turkish legations also occurred in Paris, Brussels, Geneva, Athens, and Los Angeles. The majority of these actions involved explosions, although there were also several armed attacks and a few assassinations.

During this period ASALA was organizing, and attempting to establish its place within the Armenian community and the world at large. This evidently also involved collaboration with the Palestinian terror organizations in Beirut — under whose auspices ASALA was in fact operating. This phase in ASALA's life does indeed correspond with the strategy as formulated above. Indeed, even if a strategy is itself only retroactively formulated after the first years, it nevertheless constitutes the first and essential chapter in the life of any terrorist organization.

A review of ASALA's actions during these years reveals yet another point connected with its operations inside Turkey itself. In May 1977 two explosions took place in Istanbul, and in January 1978 the refineries in Izmir were reportedly attacked. Responsibility for these attacks was claimed by an organization calling itself the "28th of May" (May 28 was the date on which the Armenian Republic was declared in 1918). Conceivably these attacks were connected with an effort on the part of ASALA to bring the violent struggle home to the Armenian population in Turkey, most if not all of whom lived in the big cities. In any case no popular movement, or even isolated Armenian terror cells, were established in Turkey. Considering that during those years Turkey was swept by waves of terror from both the right and the left, and none of the government's efforts to maintain law and order proved to be a deterrent, the absence of Armenian terror can only be connected with the climate prevailing among the Armenian community there. With the exception of an explosion at Ankara airport in May 1979, and an explosion at the airport of Istanbul in December of the same year, no ASALA attacks were registered in Turkey until another attack on Ankara airport in August 1982.

Expanding the Scope of Attacks

The year 1979 was a turning point for ASALA, and involved a number of important changes in its modus operandi. The trends that emerged at that time have continued to this day: a significant increase in the frequency of attacks, the strengthening of links between ASALA and other terrorist organizations, and in particular the shift to attacks on non-Turkish targets.

Nature of the attacks: As already mentioned, only a limited number of attacks was carried out during each of the years before 1978. In contrast, 13 attacks took place in 1979, 34 in 1980, 49 in 1981, and 24 during 1982. The decline in the level of activity in 1982, following a steady increase during the preceding three years, is explained by yet another characteristic of ASALA's activities in the past few years: its tendency to increase the frequency of its attacks during the closing months of the year: of the 13 actions ASALA carried out in 1979, only four took place prior to the end of September. Of the 33 attacks during 1980, only five were carried out before the end of September. And only 21 of the 49 attacks during 1981 took place before the end of September. No explanation has been found for this phenomenon, which is even stranger in light of the fact that most of the memorial days of the Armenian nation in general, and of ASALA in particular, occur during the first half of the year. In 1982 ASALA carried out 24 attacks; most of these occurred before the end of September. But by that time the evacuation of Beirut by the terrorist organizations had taken place, and this drastically influenced ASALA's activities, at least temporarily.

The majority of actions involved two specific tactics: murder and explosive attacks. The targets of the assassination attempts all over the world were without exception Turkish diplomats. The attacks were carried out with great precision by lone assailants, or by groups of two, who always managed to cover their tracks before leaving the scene of the attack. Bomb attacks were also carried out against non-Turkish targets and, judging by their timing and matter of execution, were evidently directed against property without intent to kill. Most of these attacks were executed with equal precision and professional skill, although with the steep increase in the frequency of the attacks, a certain decrease in the level of proficiency became noticeable: after 1980 increasing numbers of ASALA members were caught, apart from which several mishaps occurred when explosive charges went off prematurely.

The occupation of the Turkish Embassy in Paris (September 24, 1981) was ASALA's first siege-hostage operation. Judging from the absence of specific demands by the attackers, and from the rather hasty manner in which the leader of the action abandoned it to seek medical treatment, it may be concluded that the attack was mainly intended for publicity purposes, rather than to satisfy some specific demand. During this same period ASALA displayed a capacity to carry out simultaneous attacks in different, widely removed places. On October 5, 1980, for instance, the Alitalia office in Madrid was bombed, and on the same day a bomb blast took place at the Turkish Consulate in Los Angeles. On August 20, 1981, explosions took place simultaneously in the offices of a Swiss company in Los Angeles, and at the Alitalia offices in Paris. There were a few more cases of simultaneous explosions in the same city: on October 23, 1981, two explosions took place in Paris, followed by similar incidents on November 16, 1981, and July 20, 1982. Moreover, on a number of occasions different targets in one and the same city were hit only days apart. The simultaneous nature of the attacks confirms assumptions about centralized planning and the existence of a command center which controls the actions of the various ASALA groups.

Operational cooperation with other organizations: ASALA developed a ramified network of contacts with other terror organizations, but operationally this has manifested itself in only a few isolated cases. On November 10, 1980, the organization, together with the Kurdish Labor Party (KLP), claimed responsibility for an explosion at the Turkish Consulate in Strasbourg; an explosion at the Turkish tourist office in Rome, which occurred the next day, was also claimed by the two. With the exception of these two attacks, only one other case is known where the organization is certain to have cooperated with another terror group: at the beginning of August 1982 the Turkish authorities frustrated a planned PLO attack on Israeli and Jewish targets in Istanbul, that apparently was intended to coincide with an ASALA attack on Ankara airport, which indeed took place on August 7, 1982.

The shift to attacks on western targets, which occurred during this period, has a significance beyond demonstrating ASALA's capability to expand the scope of its activities. In addition to the direct threat resulting from this development, it touches on issues concerning the organization's policy and strategy. The change first became apparent on September 13, 1979, following a number of explosions at the offices of KLM, Lufthansa, and Turkish Airlines in Paris. It is difficult to say whether this extension of the scope of the targets was planned in advance, or whether a justification was invented retroactively and placed in a strategic revolutionary context. In any event, the change raises a question regarding the centrality of the leftist "anti-imperialist" motivation in ASALA's ideology.

Although the attacks concerned western targets, they took place within a limited and consistent framework, with regard both to the type of attacks, and the choice of targets. The only actions against western (or other) targets which could not be justified by any direct link with ASALA were a series of explosions at the British, Italian, and American tourist offices in Paris on November 25, 1979; the explosions at the Iranian, British, Israeli, Philippine, and American tourist offices in Rome on December 9, 1979; the explosions at the American and French tourist offices on December 23, 1979 — again in Rome; the explosions near the American, Swiss, and Belgian tourist offices on January 19, 1980, in Madrid; and the last incidents in this series, which occurred on February 18, 1980, when the Israeli, German, and Swiss tourist offices in Rome were bombed. But the subsequent announcements by ASALA, as in previous years, contained a clear anti-imperialist message, while simultaneously the organization's contacts with other leftist — in particular Palestinian — organizations were reinforced.

Even if these ideological declarations are accepted as authentic, the shift to attacks on western targets is not in keeping with the organization's strategic platform as embodied in its policy declarations, i.e., that it forms an integral part of the international revolution. The attacks by ASALA on western targets, in the absence of any direct provocation by the countries they represent, seem altogether too arbitrary. If western targets were attacked merely because they were "reactionary," it might be assumed that the attacks would, at least in part, be concentrated on diplomatic targets. But here the targets hit were commercial, and the reason was almost certainly the existence of tourist relations with Turkey. This is confirmed by the fact that ASALA's declarations consistently stress the West's relations and cooperation with the "fascist" regime in Turkey.

Any cases where countries arrested Armenian terrorists were

similarly construed as cooperation with Turkey, and from 1980 onwards such arrests have led to waves of attacks against western countries. This trend has been pursued consistently up to the present day. Yet most of these actions involved ASALA groups using aliases, such as the "9th of June Organization" and the "Orly Group," and ASALA subsequently published a denial of any connection with them. This policy does not jibe with a trend of attacking western targets, but rather reveals an effort to disguise ASALA's involvement in anti-western terror.

Until the middle of 1982 ASALA's activities as a terror organization reflected growing strength and a systematic policy, both in choice of targets and in methods of operation (even if their practical expressions did not match the declared strategy). All this took place with hardly any external interference until, following the Lebanon War and the elimination of its main base in Beirut, the organization was confronted with the need to adjust to a different set of external and internal conditions.

ASALA's Activities from 1982 Onwards: Escalation and Crisis

On August 7, 1982, ASALA carried out a suicide attack at Esenboga Airport in Ankara. This action, which caused dozens of civilian casualties, including nine killed, signified an escalation aimed at the indiscriminate harming of human life — an inevitable consequence of actions of this kind. Actually, the beginnings of a shift to aselective terror had been observed a few weeks earlier: on July 20, 1982, two explosions took place in Paris, followed four days later by another explosion. In all three cases the targets ASALA chose were Turkish tourist offices in central locations and the attacks resulted in casualties among civilian passersby. (In contrast, in the series of attacks on tourist offices in centrally-located European cities carried out during 1979-80, the explosions were timed for nighttime, and were not expressly intended to cause civilian casualties.) The first signs of escalation could also have been discerned one year previously, during the occupation of the Turkish Consulate in Paris in September 1981. Notwithstanding these, the significance of the attack on Ankara airport lay in its spectacular scope.

This attack must be seen as the culmination of the processes to which ASALA had been subjected in the course of its evolution, and as such must probably be considered a consequence of the new conditions under which the organization was forced to operate at this time. The Lebanon War in the summer of 1982 had affected all the non-Palestinian terror organizations that were logistically and operationally dependent upon the Palestinian organizations in Lebanon, with ASALA a prime example. ASALA had established itself in Beirut under the patronage of the PLO, and was known to maintain links with the PFLP, the Democratic Front for the Liberation of Palestine (DFLP), and Fatah. The war caused ASALA to lose its logistic strongholds in Lebanon, even if only for a few months — forcing it to concentrate on the preservation of its unity and the restoration of its operational capabilities.

The elimination of ASALA's Beirut headquarters naturally also affected its European operational centers. The consequences were particularly evident during the months immediately following the evacuation: until the middle of 1983 ASALA carried out only incidental attacks; these were directed against Turkish targets, and were apparently organized with the aid of the existing European infrastructure. On January 22, 1983, an explosion at a Turkish tourist office in Paris was narrowly averted; that same day a Turkish tourist office elsewhere in Paris was attacked. On February 28, 1983, a bomb was discovered at the residence of a Turkish diplomat in Luxembourg, while on the same day an explosion occurred at a Turkish tourist office in Paris. These simultaneous attacks were clearly not the spontaneous efforts of groups of irregulars, but rather indicate that the organization almost certainly still possessed a central command structure — possibly the very same one that had existed earlier in Beirut, now relocated elsewhere. Apart from this, there were increasing reports about a reorganization of ASALA as well as a search for new bases in Greece, the Greek sector of Cyprus, and eventually also in Syria and Iran. From hereon, ASALA manifestos began to arrive from Athens,[23] from Damascus, but also from Los Angeles,[24] though Beirut's communications services continued to be used.

As mentioned before, the crisis which hit ASALA following the evacuation of Beirut resulted in a need for new operational bases. Prior to its attack on Orly Airport ASALA organized a logistics support network in Paris, for which purpose Hagop Hagopian arrived there. This base was seriously hit when, following the attack, the Paris police raided the homes of Armenian activists in Paris, arrested some 50 persons, and seized large caches of arms and ammunition. Most of those arrested were released after a short while, and only 11 were indicted for terrorist activities.[25] Through mid-1985 ASALA had not resumed its operations on French soil, although it could be assumed that this was a temporary cessation connected with the need for reorganization, and not necessarily a consequence of French deterrent successes. The organization carried out a series of attacks against French targets on Iranian territory during July and August 1983, in continuance of its well-known policy of pressuring western nations which have arrested its members.

The operational level of the attacks carried out in Iran, as well as that of the explosion at the French diplomatic mission in West Berlin on August 25, 1983, reinforce a growing impression, particularly since the Lebanon War, of a decline in ASALA's ability to carry out sophisticated attacks. The attacks in Europe during the period preceding the explosion at Orly Airport showed a low level of operational proficiency, even though the planning as such was not easy. A critical review of the organization's activities from July 1983 till mid-1985 strongly suggests a similar decline in the level of personnel chosen to carry out the attacks. The reason for this was, almost certainly, too hasty recruitment resulting from a desire to carry out attacks quickly and at any price, in order to "stay on the map," even if the operational level were impaired as a result.

The dramatic attack on Orly Airport on July 15, 1983, demonstrated a tendency toward escalation in the organization's activities, and reflected the extended time it had required since the summer of 1982 to reorganize itself for more sophisticated actions. It was also related to yet another significant date. On July 22, 1983, the 11th session of the Armenian National Congress opened in Lausanne, and this event spurred the members of the extreme wing to prove ASALA's existence in the eyes of the world, and particularly the Armenian community. This was their answer to the adherents of non-violent, political struggle.

In a similar vein, we must ask whether the recourse to spectacular actions such as the attack on Ankara airport was not an indication of ASALA's desire to prove its continued existence, and its capacity to strike at this particular time, however fraught with organizational and logistic difficulties — not only to Turkey, but to Armenians throughout the world and the international com-

29

munity as well. There is no doubt that this action, which made headlines worldwide, served this purpose. But today it is possible, on the basis of documentation and witness reports that have been collected since then, to connect the demonstrative action in Ankara with another, far more significant and compelling reason.

ASALA has since its inception been subject to two central motivations. The first called for limiting attacks to Turkish objectives, as the principal targets of the organization, while the second pulled in the direction of joining the international revolutionary struggle.[26] In the course of the years the extremist tendency found expression in ASALA's ideological and strategic declarations, which appear to have received the support of a significant section of the membership and leaders of the organization. But apparently another, less vocal but nevertheless dominant section, held that the organization should restrict itself to a more limited range of targets. This may explain the apparent gap between ASALA's declared strategic platform and its actual policy. The call for alignment with the international revolutionary struggle may be explained by another fact closely connected with ASALA's very existence: logistics dependence (and possibly even a certain degree of operational cooperation) between ASALA and the Palestinian organizations. This cooperation was of course also imposed by an absence of choice: like other organizations lacking political connections and the means of exercising pressure, ASALA was, from the day of its establishment, in need of the protection and backing of groups stronger than itself. Even so there seems no doubt that a leftist ideological consensus between those who extend the patronage, and the leading group within ASALA, was and continues to be authentic. The escalation in the attacks, and the shift to activities in which neutral bystanders were liable to get hurt, has been the almost inevitable outcome of this ideological orientation.

During the same period in which this polarization of opinions manifested itself, there almost certainly occurred an aggravation of the differences of opinion between the proponents of escalation and the more moderate streams within the organization. This was a consequence of the sudden need in the summer of 1982 to decide upon ASALA's future course. Against this backdrop a split occurred within the organizations's leadership — the ramifications of which are not yet entirely clear. It is known, however, that an extreme faction stayed close to the Palestinian bodies and moved with them to training camps in Syria and the Lebanese Beka'a, which is under Syrian domination. Another, more moderate group resigned from the organization and moved to Europe out of fear lest ASALA become a tool of the Syrian and Palestinian forces.[27] This group, calling itself the Armenian Revolutionary Movement, formally denounced ASALA following the attack on Orly Airport on July 15, 1983, and distributed a manifesto complaining against the leadership and extremist attitude of Hagop Hagopian. According to the Armenian Revolutionary Movement the Armenian struggle has to remain focused against Turkey, and to be transferred to Turkish territory, there to rely on local opponents of the regime, such as the Kurdish minority. At one point the internal conflict reached a point where the opposing factions traded gunshots, and the secessionists were accused by ASALA of being "lackeys in the service of Turkish imperialism and the CIA."[28]

Today, then, Asala is faced with a number of fundamental problems: the rebuilding of a logistics and human infrastructure for the organization, and the need to confront internal conflicts and factional divisions. Moreover, the organization must confront the revised strength of the proponents of political struggle among the international Armenian community. Nevertheless, in light of the ideological and operational trends which have characterized the organization during the last few years, and in view of the growing polarization of Armenian attitudes, the threat ASALA poses for Turkey and the western nations still exists. One key feature underpinning this reality is ASALA's connections with international terror.

IV. Asala's Structure

Internal Structure and Organizational Foundations

ASALA is a closely-knit organization, and is particularly difficult to penetrate due to the extreme homogeneity of its human
infrastructure. Information about the organization's internal
structure does not originate from primary sources, but has been
induced from its operational characteristics since it first appeared
on the scene. The resulting picture is that of a highly-centralized
organization. This centralized control is a function of ASALA's
relatively small size and secret character, and possibly also of the
personal qualities of its leadership. In recent years only a few
names have been mentioned of personalities in the upper echelons
of ASALA who could be considered responsible for determining its
operational policies. ASALA leaders are involved in activities at
various levels, from decisionmaking to operations, except perhaps
active participation in the attacks themselves.

This centralization, as well as the close involvement of only a
limited number of activists, enables close supervision by the
leadership of the objectives of attack and the organization's
operatives, and at one time also of ASALA's tight geographical
organization. Even so, the organization's centralized structure
appears to have been influenced by additional factors which were
not so much connected with the ASALA framework as such, as with
a sympathetically disposed environment. Until the evacuation of
West Beirut by the terrorist organizations, ASALA's headquarters
there enjoyed freedom of action under the protection of the PLO.
Hagop Hagopian, who has been introduced as the organization's
spokesman, and who probably has the deciding voice in ASALA's
Central Committee, had his headquarters in Beirut. There,
apparently, all training as well as organizational and operational
activities were also concentrated. In July 1982 a member of the
"Orly Group" (which belongs to ASALA) was arrested in Paris.
According to his testimony, operational instructions for the group
were received by telephone from Beirut.[29] However, there is also no
doubt that the large Armenian community in France serves as a
logistics base for the coordination of operations in Europe,
especially in France.

Conjecture about the organization's centralized structure, and the close ties between the various links in the European network and their Beirut headquarters, is supported by the fact that the first few months following the PLO's departure from Beirut showed a marked decline in ASALA's activities. Evidently the evacuation had produced organizational, operational and logistics problems for ASALA, as well as for the Palestinian groups. Following the evacuation the operational bases were apparently dispersed, although somewhat later some of its leadership returned to Beirut,[30] while a training base for ASALA operatives was established in the Lebanese Beka'a Valley (which is under Syrian domination),[31] and a reorganization was carried out in the Middle East and Europe. In mid-1985 other ASALA groups could be found in Iran[32] and Syria.[33]

Immediately following the evacuation of Beirut, an ASALA training center was organized in the Greek sector of Cyprus, while simultaneously another, apparently political, base was established in Greece.[34] Another European center was situated in Paris, as reflected in the fact that several weeks before the explosion at the Turkish Airlines counter at Orly Airport (July 15, 1983), a "logistics support group" was established there. This group is said to have had the backing of a previously existing operational infrastructure composed of members of the local Armenian population, although in this case too, several of the operatives arrived from Athens.[35]

Thus, despite the changes resulting from the dispersion of ASALA's operational bases, no significant change took place in the nature of its leadership — at least not with regard to its European groups — and the organization remained highly centralized, and dominated by only a small number of people. By the nature of things, however, it is very difficult to judge the degree of independence of the groups residing in Syria and Iran, or the character of their relationship with each other and the central leadership. The answer may lie in the nature of the connections between the organization's headquarters and the countries concerned, but for the time being this question remains open.

Apart from the above-mentioned main bases, ASALA reportedly maintained a number of — apparently operational — cells in various other locations around the world: in Europe — Denmark, Switzerland, Italy, Spain, France, Germany, and Austria; the United States and Venezuela on the American continent; Libya in the Middle East; and Australia.[36]

Attribution

ASALA's activities, consisting mainly of assassinations and bomb attacks, are carried out by very small squads, comprising not more than two to four ASALA members. At times ASALA gives these squads a nom de guerre for a particular operation; the names chosen are intended to commemorate members who were killed or executed.

— The Suicide Commando of Yachia Kecmicmean (Kesnishian). On September 24, 1981, this group attacked the Turkish Consulate in Paris.

— Martyr Kharmian Suicide Squad/ Pierre Gulumian Suicide Squad. Following the attack at Ankara airport on August 7, 1982, telephone calls were received using these names to claim responsibility.

— Levon Ekmekcian Commando. Under this name responsibility was claimed for the attack at the Istanbul bazaar on June 21, 1983.

Other groups have been called after their place of origin:

— ASALA: The Los Angeles Branch.

— ASALA: The Toronto Branch.

Apart from the above cases, ASALA has used certain names to take responsibility for a large number of actions. Here sub-groups were formed within the organization with closely defined targets. These are cases in which ASALA acted systematically, in reaction to the arrest of some of its members, by means of fictitiously-named groups called after a specific country, place or date connected with the arrest.

— 3rd of October Movement. On October 3, 1980, two ASALA members were arrested after an explosive charge they were handling in a Geneva hotel room blew up. The two, Alex Yenikomishian, and Suzy Memserdjian, were released on January 12 and 9, 1981, respectively. While the two were under arrest, and even after their release, ASALA continued to carry out attacks against Swiss targets under this name.

— 9th of June Organization. On June 9, 1981, an ASALA member, Mardiros Jamgotchian, was arrested while attacking a Turkish diplomat in Geneva. This signaled the start of an additional wave of attacks on Swiss targets.

— Swiss 15 Group. Under this name ASALA claimed responsibility for attacks on Swiss targets. The activities of the group began after a Swiss court had sentenced Jamgotchian to a 15-year prison sentence. (The trial started on December 15, 1981.)

— Orly Group. Under this name ASALA claimed responsibility for attacks on French targets following the arrest of one of its members, Monte Melkonian, at Orly Airport in November 1981. Despite his release in December of the same year, the attacks on French targets continued. As justification, ASALA cited the arrest of four organization members following the occupation of the Turkish Consulate in Paris in September 1981, before the appearance of the Orly Group. Not only has the Orly Group been the most active among the revenge cells established by ASALA, but it has carried out attacks on non-French targets, such as Turkish legations.

— September France. This is a name used by ASALA to claim responsibility for attacks on French targets. The name was probably inspired by the occupation of the Turkish Embassy in Paris, which took place on September 24, 1981.

A detailed list of Armenian organizations, some of which are undoubtedly connected with ASALA, appears in Appendix 1.

Leaders and Members

Data about the ASALA leadership, both as regards their place in the organizational hierarchy and their personal antecedents, are very scarce. The available scraps of information are sketchy, and even contradictory. According to Turkish sources, the Central Committee of the organization consists of four members:[37] Hagop Hagopian, Antranik Bagosian, Onnik Basmacian, and Bagos Turbaclian.

It is safe to assume that some, or even all of these names are pseudonyms, and that their owners will turn up in different places under different names. Of these four, at any rate, details are known only about Hagop Hagopian.

In December 1980 Hagop Hagopian introduced himself as the head of ASALA to the Armenian newspaper *Hay Baykar,* which is published in Paris. In September 1981 ASALA organized a press conference in Beirut, at which Hagop Hagopian was introduced as the organization's spokesman. During his conversation with the newsmen his face was covered. At the end of July 1982 Hagop Hagopian was reported killed during an Israeli artillery bombardment on Beirut. His death was confirmed by another ASALA leader, Mihran Mihranian,[38] but subsequently it was claimed that Mihranian was in itself a pseudonym of Hagopian.[39] Thus the information about Hagopian's death may have been false, and intended to enable him to go underground. The possibility gained credibility in light of the fact that not a single action or commando unit was ever named after him, while activists of far lower rank than Hagopian had previously been memorialized in this way. Moreover, the news of Hagopian's death was never confirmed by independent sources, and ASALA never carried out any acts of revenge against Israeli targets even though — if ASALA's claims were to be believed — Hagopian was killed by an Israeli bombardment. It is not surprising, therefore, that Hagopian reportedly re-emerged in February and April 1983 in Paris,[40] where he was said to have participated in the creation of a logistics framework for ASALA, as well as the planning of the explosion at Orly Airport on July 15, 1983. In March 1983, during the period Hagopian was said to be dead, the ASALA leader Mihran Mihranian conducted a press visit to the organization's base in the Beka'a Valley in Lebanon.[41]

There is some reason to believe that Hagop Hagopian is the pseudonym of a young Armenian of aristocratic birth, known in Bourj el-Hamud, the Armenian district of Beirut, by the name of Abu Mujahed. He is said to have shown a natural gift for leadership, and to have been chosen as the head of ASALA as far back as 1975. He is believed to be in his thirties.[42] In August 1982, again during the period that Hagopian was believed dead, an interview with Abu Mujahed representing ASALA was published in Lebanon,[43] while during June 1983 Abu Mujahed was reported to have conducted a press tour "somewhere in Lebanon."[44] On the strength of the above, it seems fairly certain that Abu Mujahed, Mihranian, and Hagopian are in fact one and the same person.

Hagop Hagopian is believed to hold extremist views with regard to the methods through which ASALA's struggle should be conducted. Those who have left the organization have accused him of being a "dictator and a gangster," due to the way in which he forces the organization to engage in propaganda attacks without any consideration for the targets or the resulting toll in human life.[45] Hagop Hagopian's permanent domicile is unknown. In September 1983 he was said to be in Libya,[46] while in May 1984 a source in the American Federal Bureau of Investigation claimed that he lived in Damascus.[47]

Regarding ASALA's membership almost nothing is known. Very few members have been caught relative to the number of actions carried out by ASALA, despite the fact that most were perpetrated in broad daylight and in crowded streets. The organization itself has from the very day of its foundation maintained secrecy by sealing itself off from the outside world. Any information supplied to the news media is restricted to ideological declarations and bulletins about intended actions. From information collected over the years, it appears that ASALA members belong predominantly to middle-class Armenian families living in Lebanon, the United States, and France. The emigration of Armenians from Turkey and Iran has continued during recent years, and it is quite possible that, apart from those belonging to families who left Turkey three generations ago, the organization relies on youngsters who are newly arrived in the West. According to ASALA, there are no foreigners in its ranks; independent observation appears to confirm this contention. The age of ASALA members varies from 20-30 years, and the membership includes a number of women.

According to a Turkish source, ASALA aims at becoming a popular movement, and to this end recruits youngsters of Armenian origin, mainly students in Beirut.[48] This approach, however, would appear to contradict ASALA's objective of being a small and secret organization, as well as its methods of operation. At any rate, this contention is not supported by any other source, although the claim regarding recruitment of members of the organization at the universities in Beirut does seem plausible. There is no doubt that this important source of manpower for the continued existence of the organization was severely affected as a result of the Lebanon War and the evacuation of Beirut.

Estimates about the strength of ASALA's membership are equally incomplete and contradictory. The figures vary from several hundreds (the highest estimate being about one thousand persons[49]) to several dozens.[50] The latter would appear to be the more reliable. According to the organization itself, in early 1985 some 85 of its members were imprisoned in Great Britain, France, Switzerland, Italy and Canada, a claim which would appear to be exaggerated. According to a Turkish source, 25 ASALA members were detained at this time outside Turkey, and this estimate would seem to be more reasonable.

Prominent ASALA Activists

A study of the most prominent activists in ASALA fails to yield much information that can help to raise the curtain of secrecy in which the organization is shrouded. Any known details are derived from events and actions with which they were connected, and that tells us little about the place of those involved in the organization's hierarchy, or — in most cases — about their personal background.

— *Keshishian* is said to be in charge of ASALA's training camps in the Trodos mountains in the Greek sector of Cyprus. He is a former Armenian priest, who was trained by the PFLP. According to Turkish sources he is connected with a Turkish Marxist-Leninist group called Halk Yontemi ("People's Method").[51]

— *Monte Melkonian,* an ASALA nom de guerre, is also known as Katchig Averdissian, and Hachik Averfian. Melkonian was arrested at Orly Airport in November 1981. A false Cypriot passport in the name of Dimitrio Giorgio was found in his possession. He was released by the French authorities on January 12, 1982.

— *Alexander (Ara Alex) Yenikomishian* (Ara Komchovian) was arrested on October 3, 1980 in Geneva, together with Suzy

— Memserdjian, after an explosive charge he was handling in his hotel room blew up prematurely. He lost his eyesight in the explosion. Yenikomishian was released in January 1981, to be welcomed upon his arrival in Beirut by a delegation of the PFLP.

— *Keorek Vartanian* was in charge of the heroin smuggling network operated by ASALA with Palestinian participation, which was exposed by the Swedish authorities in November 1981.

— *Dr. Hratch Lousinian* was, according to some reports, one of the senior leaders of ASALA. He was killed in a car accident in western Syria in 1982. Lousinian studied at Yerevan University in Soviet Armenia for seven years.[52]

V. Asala and International Terrorism

Throughout the years since ASALA's establishment, reports and testimonies have accumulated about its connections with other bodies — both terrorist organizations and states. According to these sources, ASALA maintains an international network of ties in three fields: ideological, logistic, and operational.

Underlying the creation of this network are the following two main factors: from a practical point of view, ASALA's lack of its own national territory and — as a result — material resources, bases, and political strength, has made it from the day of its inception dependent upon the protection and support of bodies stronger than itself. The second factor is ideological. ASALA has a leftist orientation, and the organization's manifestos emphasize that the Armenian question forms a part of the international revolution. This world view, in effect, automatically results in solidarity with other leftist groups.

Even so, the evidence about ASALA's international connections — e.g., information about its ties with other terrorist organizations — is often contradictory and unreliable. All such information should, in fact, be scrutinized in light of the fact that governments or other bodies are at times interested in creating the impression of the existence of closely-knit and menacing international terrorist connections. Although they probably contain a kernel of truth, some of the reports must nevertheless be deemed exaggerated. On the other hand, denials by terrorist organizations, including ASALA, of their external connections are usually intended to allay any suspicion that they depend on the support of an outside body, state or terrorist organization, as this might undermine the authenticity and credibility of their own struggle.

Connections with Terrorist Organizations

The most reliable evidence about ASALA's connections with other terrorist organizations comes from a first-hand source: according to Mihran Mihranian (i.e., apparently, Hagop Hagopian), its revolutionary experience taught ASALA that every organization had to establish relations with other like-minded organizations; hence, ASALA sought to establish a connection with freedom movements in the Middle East.[53]

ASALA is indeed known to maintain connections with Palestinian organizations, leftist Turkish organizations, and Kurdish organizations — the latter also in Turkey. These ties have evolved beyond ideological solidarity, and their quality and intensity show that they serve a function in their own right.

Ties with Palestinian organizations. Despite denials by Arafat[54] and Abu Firas,[55] who was the PLO representative in Ankara, it seems that both logistic and operational ties exist between ASALA and the Palestinian organizations. There is detailed evidence regarding ASALA's connections with the PLO. In particular, links have been developed with Fatah, the Popular Front for the Liberation of Palestine (PFLP) headed by George Habash, and Naif Hawatme's Democratic Front for the Liberation of Palestine (DFLP). Since ASALA's foundation in 1975, the PLO has acted as its patron and organizational model, and from the outset ASALA's headquarters were situated in Beirut in the area controlled by the PLO. ASALA's first press conference, held on November 9, 1978 in Beirut, took place in an area under PFLP control.

Numerous sources have reported on ASALA members being trained under the aegis of Fatah; some refer specifically to training at Hamuriah, Fatah's training facility in Syria, as when, in the course of 1979, 130 Armenian terrorists underwent training there.[56] The four ASALA operatives who attacked the Turkish Embassy in Paris (September 24, 1981) originated reportedly from Lebanon, where they were trained by the Palestinians.[57] Similarly, the squad which attacked Ankara airport on August 7, 1982, was reportedly trained at Hamuriah.[58]

ASALA's connection with the PFLP also involved training assistance and, according to reports, ASALA members were for a number of years trained by the "Front" in Lebanon, South Yemen, and Syria.[59] Additional sources report that ASALA operatives were trained by the DFLP.[60] It is almost certain that the Palestinian organizations have also assisted ASALA with the supply of weapons and other logistics, even though most of the evidence in this regard is of an indirect nature. Thus, for a number of years George Habash's PFLP reportedly supplied the Armenians (presumably ASALA) with sabotage materials and weapons, in addition to printing leaflets for them.[61] During the attack on Ankara airport, the ASALA operatives used a Polish WZ-63 9mm submachine gun that was presumed to be of Palestinian or Syrian origin.[62] Moreover, according to other reports, ASALA received PLO weapons both in Beirut and at the transfer point in Nicosia, during the evacuation of Beirut in September 1982.[63]

In July 1982, an explosion occurred in a villa in Paris when Pierre Gulumian, a member of the Orly Group, was handling an explosive charge. A police investigation revealed that the house was also used as a Palestinian arms depot.[64] This may indeed have been a joint depot, either under the control of, or used together with other parties, and serving ASALA together with various Palestinian groups in Europe. In another case, in November 1981 an ASALA member named Monte Melkonian was arrested in Paris on suspicion of being involved in the bomb attack on the Antwerp synagogue in October of that year. His false Cypriot passport, in the name of Dimitrio Giorgio, belonged to the same numerical series as that used by "Alexander Panadry," the principal suspect in the explosion at the synagogue on Rue Copernique in Paris on October 3, 1980.[65] In this connection, counterfeit Cypriot passports were reported to have been supplied to ASALA by the DFLP.[66] According to another source, ASALA had itself printed false Turkish passports in Beirut, which were distributed to other, not necessarily Armenian, terrorist groups. This reference is almost certainly to Palestinian organizations.[67]

Another area of cooperation between ASALA and the Palestinians is drug smuggling, a means increasingly employed by terrorist organizations in order to raise funds needed for financing their operations. In 1981 a drug smuggling network was discovered in Sweden. According to police sources, it was organized by the PLO, but employed numerous Armenians, and the vast sums of money that passed through its hands were used mainly for arms purchases. One of the members of the network, an Armenian called George Mahluf (almost certainly a pseudonym), was tried in Sweden at the end of 1983.[68]

Very little information exists about cooperation between ASALA and Palestinian organizations in actual operations. Such a possibility was raised in November 1980, after a Syrian and a Lebanese arrested in Switzerland told their interrogators that they had been sent from Beirut to carry out attacks on behalf of the Armenian underground.[69] It is indeed a fact that during that period ASALA was carrying out intensive attacks against Swiss targets, but in this specific case it is more probable that ASALA undertook attacks on behalf of Palestinian organizations, in recognition of their support, rather than the reverse possibility. Further evidence in this regard is of a later date: during the Israeli siege of Beirut in the summer of 1982, ASALA supporters reportedly fought side by side with Palestinians in the western part of the city.[70] At the same time ASALA functionaries reportedly met with PFLP leaders for joint planning sessions.[71] According to another source, during the same period ASALA was expected to render practical assistance to the PLO, and the organizations agreed upon joint actions, such as airplane hijackings and attacks in Turkey and Europe.[72] This allegation is supported by evidence about operational cooperation between ASALA and the PLO. In the week that the attack on Ankara airport took place (August 7, 1982), three Palestinians carrying false passports, who turned out to be PLO members, were arrested in Istanbul, in possession of a map indicating the location of the El Al offices in the city, as well as a list with the names of twenty Jewish residents of Istanbul.[73] This led to the assumption that the PLO had intended to hit Jewish targets in the city simultaneously with the ASALA action in Ankara. (As with other cases, first-hand evidence to support this suspicion is lacking, although the assumption seems plausible.)

Reports from the second half of 1983 tell of the connections that developed between ASALA and the Fatah Revolutionary Council (FRC), better known as the Abu Nidal Group. Most of these reports are lacking in detail about the nature of the connection, but according to some, ASALA provided shelter in Paris to the group which attacked the Goldenberg restaurant in the city in August 1982,[74] an event which was attributed to the Abu Nidal Group.

A certain ambivalence was evidently introduced into relations between ASALA and the PLO after the opening of a PLO office in Ankara in October 1979. There is no doubt that this step was hardly to ASALA's liking, but its protests — if there were any — would hardly have affected the pragmatic political considerations guiding the PLO. The present rapprochement between ASALA and the Abu Nidal Group may conceivably be seen against the back-drop of ASALA's increasing ties with Syria, and the rise of radical forces within ASALA, parallel with a significant weakening in the PLO's strength since the summer of 1982, which reduced its ability to support or influence other organizations.

Links with leftist Lebanese organizations. It was only natural that connections would be established between ASALA and other Lebanese groups with closely related ideological attitudes. Thus, ASALA reportedly maintained contact with the Lebanese Arab

Army (LAA), a militant group supported by Libya. A press conference convened by ASALA (probably the first one, of November 9, 1978) was reportedly held in the cellar of the Voice of the Arab Revolution radio station and the Workers News Agency, both connected with the LAA.[75] On that occasion it was announced that all future contacts with ASALA would be conducted via the *Al Shaghyla* news agency (established by Libya).[76] Another, smaller, leftist Lebanese militia with which ASALA maintained contact is the Workers League, founded by Khatib al-Zahir and his brother Thaker. ASALA activists trained together with members of this group in the mountain regions of Lebanon under the personal direction of Khatib, in addition to which ASALA was allocated airtime on the militia's radio programs. This group's links with terror are unclear, but its offices, as well as its radio station are reportedly situated in the Palestinian-controlled areas of Lebanon.[77]

Links with leftist Turkish organizations. The sentence "Long Live the Armenian, Kurdish and Turkish Struggle" appeared in a manifesto issued by ASALA following the explosion at the Turkish Embassy in Toronto on January 14, 1982.

Links between ASALA and Turkish and Kurdish underground organizations stem to a certain extent from a shared ideological basis, but mainly from the fact that all have a common enemy — Turkey and its present regime. These ties exist, notwithstanding a legacy of generations of hatred among these peoples. Turkish police sources issue frequent reports on these connections, and in fact stamp all leftist organizations of any importance in present-day Turkey as being connected in one way or another with ASALA (although in the majority of cases the nature of these ties is not explained). Among the organizations mentioned are the Apoist, or Kurdish Labor Party (KLP), a leftist Kurdish organization. Before the revolution in Turkey in September 1980, this organization allegedly supplied false Turkish passports to the terrorist organizations in Beirut. The source does not mention which organizations were involved, and it may well be that ASALA also benefited from this arrangement, in exchange for which the KLP received passports of various other nationalities.[78]

A Kurdish leader revealed in 1982 that KLP members were trained by ASALA operatives in sabotage and terror methods in Palestinian camps in Lebanon.[79] According to other information, contacts were established with the aim of merging ASALA with the leftist Turkish Marxist-Leninist Armed Propaganda Unit (MLAPU).[80] One of the ASALA leaders, Keshishian, was reported in 1982 to be in touch with the leftist Turkish Halk Yonemi[81] organization, but here, too, details as to the nature of these contacts are missing. Another organization alleged to have connections with ASALA is the Turkish Communist Labor Party (TKEP), headed by Teslim Tore.[82] According to recent reports, the ASALA facilities in Paris were also used by the Kurds,[83] and members of leftist Kurdish and Turkish organizations took part in ASALA training exercises in Syrian camps.[84] In addition, ASALA allegedly has established connections with the Turkish Workers and Peasant Liberation Army.[85]

In contrast to the numerous reports about contacts on a general level between ASALA and leftist Turkish organizations — for the most part derived from the Turkish press, which does not always excel in objectivity — there is very little information about operational cooperation among these groups. In fact, only one case of actual operational cooperation is known, involving ASALA and the Kurdish KLP. At a press conference in Beirut in April 1980, leaders of the two organizations announced that they had concluded a cooperation agreement.[86] The first joint operation (according to an ASALA release) was an explosion at the Turkish Consulate in Strasbourg, France on November 10, 1980. The second, which took place the following day, was an explosion at a Turkish travel agency in Rome. No further cases of operational cooperation between ASALA and the KLP have been reported since then. There have been reports, on the other hand, of a number of murders of Turkish diplomats being planned by Armenians (probably ASALA) in cooperation with the Turkish Communist Labor Party (TKEP).[87] According to a report from December 1981, two Turkish terrorists and an (unidentified) ASALA member were arrested in London in the course of an attempt to establish contact with the Workers Voice, a group connected with the Turkish Communist Party.[88] The report adds that the trio admitted to having planned terrorist actions.

Connections with Greek-Cypriot organizations. Turkish sources claim that the Armenian struggle is supported by Cypriot Greeks (see ASALA's connections with other states, below). According to the same Turkish sources, evidence exists that Greek Cypriots have been involved in the murder of Turkish diplomats. These claims, like other claims about alleged ties among Palestinians,

Greek Cypriots, and the rightist Armenian Dashnak Party (itself connected with the JCAG), have not been substantiated. It may be assumed that they are published for propaganda purposes, as part of the ongoing controversy between Turkey and Greece. More specific reports allege ties (unspecified) between Armenians and EOKA-B (a Greek-Cypriot nationalist organization founded by General Grivas in 1971, which is effectively inactive), and Armenians and the Saloniki-based Greek Liberation Organization[89] (about which no further details are known). Still other reports speak of a meeting in Athens in April 1981 between Armenians (probably ASALA functionaries), Greek Cypriots and Kurds (whose organizational affiliation is unknown). A claim that PLO representatives also participated in this meeting, was denied by Abu-Firas, the former PLO representative in Turkey.[90] More recent reports claim that EOKA-B assisted ASALA in establishing headquarters in Nicosia, with the local security forces turning a blind eye to ASALA's activities because of its ties with EOKA.[91]

Connections with leftist European organizations. In March 1980 it was reported that German "leftist terrorists" were supplying ASALA with sabotage materials for terrorist actions in Western Europe.[92] This has not been confirmed by any other source. It seems unlikely that ASALA would require such logistics support, given that it has access to Palestinian sources of arms and ammunition, as well as a logistics support base in France. Moreover, there have never been any reports about ASALA activities in Germany or with Germans.

In an interview to the Cypriot newspaper *Al Nashara* in October 1983, the ASALA representative "did not deny the organization's connections with all groups representing the fundamental problems of their countries, such as the European New-Left and the Revolutionary Terror movements, specifically the Bader Meinhoff group (Red Army Faction) in West Germany, the French Action Directe, and the Italian Red Brigades."[93] This declaration is unsupported by other sources, and the likelihood exists that it, too, was issued mainly for propaganda purposes.

ASALA's Connections with States

Since by their very nature they possess insufficient means of their own to constitute a real threat to the regime they are fighting, terrorist organizations tend to seek out sources of outside support.

Even large organizations with considerable political clout, such as the PLO, or SWAPO (the underground movement fighting the South African government to achieve the independence of Namibia) would never have achieved their present scope without outside backing, in particular from other states. These, more than any other political bodies, are the richest sources of materiel and influence. States, for their part, have their own reasons for supporting the activities of subversive groups in other countries. Frequently, terrorist activities — that may range from mere disturbances to violent subversion with the potential to overthrow the regime — serve the interests of a foreign state. This applies particularly to cases where direct state intervention or pressures would cause troublesome or dangerous international repercussions.

Just as in the case of relations between terrorist organizations, terror groups are not interested in publicizing the assistance they receive from certain states, notwithstanding the fact that connections of this kind confer a measure of "legitimization" in international terms. As for the states involved, it is obviously difficult to expect them to admit publicly to the assistance they are giving. Such support to a group fighting another government would immediately be interpreted as intervention in the internal affairs of the other state — a situation which would produce, to say the least, an international outcry, and for which a political price might have to be paid. Thus information about states which support terror organizations, in this case ASALA, is also indirect and extremely difficult to verify on the basis of reliable sources.

ASALA is incapable of constituting a real threat to the internal stability, or even the international standing, of Turkey. Nevertheless, its struggle has indirectly become a factor in relations among the states within and beyond the region, and it is not surprising — if we may believe the reports on the subject — that the countries supporting it have their own political axe to grind with Turkey and the regional system to which it belongs.

Tensions between the USSR and Turkey must be considered within this context. Turkey is the easternmost member of NATO, and its geographical position is of the utmost strategic importance. This might explain possible direct or indirect support by the USSR for ASALA. In this case it suffices to raise the Armenian question in international forums to embarrass Turkey — quite apart from the considerable financial resources it must devote to the protection of its legations abroad. On the other hand there is little evidence of Soviet assistance to ASALA, and even this is mainly unreliable. Soviet support for ASALA may take the form of accepting Armenian terrorists at advanced training courses in terrorism and sabotage in the USSR,[94] the training of ASALA members by Soviet instructors in the PLO camp at Hamuriah in Syria,[95] and contributions of money and arms to the organization, probably through a third party — Syria or the Palestinians.[96] In light of what is known about ASALA's connections with the Palestinian movements that are known to be supported by the Soviet Union, this last piece of information is hardly remarkable except if it should be proved that the arms supplied were from the outset intended for ASALA.

Neither do declarations by ASALA functionaries contribute much to clarifying the picture. On the one hand, they categorically deny any connections with the Soviet Union; but on the other, Hagop Hagopian himself has declared that such contacts are desired by ASALA, and that the organization is working with the Soviet Union "toward an understanding that will turn Soviet Armenia into a revolutionary base from which the struggle against the fascist regime in Turkey can be conducted."[97] (Such a connection was denied by the Soviet ambassador in Ankara during a meeting with the Turkish interior minister in August 1983.[98]) Even if such support for ASALA should exist, we may safely assume that the Soviets would not allow ASALA to attempt to turn Soviet Armenia into an operational base for the organization. It is only natural that the Armenians, both those in the Soviet Union (which contains the largest concentration of Armenians in the world), and those living in other countries, look upon Soviet Armenia as their historical homeland. Soviet contacts with nationalist Armenian groups (even those, like ASALA, that consider Soviet Armenia as "liberated" territory), and the impression that the national struggle emanated from Armenia itself, would therefore be perceived by the Soviets as harming their interests, by arousing nationalist and separatist feelings among the local population. And this is exactly the situation the Soviet Union would like to avoid.

Despite this, the possibility that the Soviet Union supports ASALA indirectly — through other countries, including the East Bloc states — may not be excluded. Evidence on this score, however, must be considered in light of the reservations expressed earlier. For one, there have been reports about the supply of arms and ammunition from a Soviet source.[99] (As mentioned previously, during the attack at Ankara airport on August 7, 1982, the attackers — who belonged to ASALA — used a Polish-made WZ-63 9mm submachine gun. There is no proof that this weapon reached ASALA directly from Poland, and a more likely possibility is that it was supplied by Syria, or one of the Palestinian organizations. The same type of weapon was used in several attacks by the Abu Nidal Group, which in recent years has been supported by Syria and, even more recently, by Iraq.) The only real evidence extant concerns the training of Armenian terrorists in Syria by Bulgarian instructors,[100] but it is difficult to assess without confirmation from another source. We see, therefore, that the reports connecting the East Bloc countries with Armenian terror are few and basically speculative, although the direction in which they point makes them eminently plausible.

Assistance provided by Syria and Iran is more readily document-able. Most of it connects with ASALA's geographical reorganiza-tion since evacuating its strongholds in Beirut in September 1982, when the Palestinian organizations left the city.

We have already noted numerous reports about ASALA opera-tives being trained in the PLO's Hamuriah camp in Syria.[101] In the second half of 1983 it was reported that Armenians were reorga-nizing in new Syrian bases — this time apparently in an indepen-dent capacity, without Palestinian mediation. In this connection a large camp has been mentioned about two hours drive from Damascus, as well as camps in Kamishli (where PFLP training is conducted), Homs, and Tadmur as-Sahara[102] (it seems reasonable to assume a certain overlap in this information). There are also ASALA activists in Lebanon, in the areas under Syrian control. Armenians are reportedly being trained in a camp near the village of Anjar in the Beka'a Valley,[103] and near Tripoli in northern Lebanon, where they operate together with "Al-Fursan al-Arab," a militia founded by Rifat Assad.[104]

The possibility that ASALA has been establishing new bases in Syria connects with other reports, according to which Armenian activists who participated in terrorist attacks in Europe origin-ated from Syria. This emerged from the interrogation of an ASALA member who took part in the assassination of a Turkish diplomat in Brussels on July 14, 1983, and who was arrested in the Netherlands, as well as from the interrogation of the ASALA operative who, the following day, planted the bomb at Orly Airport in Paris.[105] Even earlier, at the height of the Lebanon War, the ASALA operatives who attacked Ankara airport on August 7, 1982, allegedly arrived in Turkey from Syria.[106]

Relations between Syria and Turkey have been difficult for a long time. Tensions derive from a number of factors, including a continual dispute over control of the waters of the Euphrates. Against this backdrop, direct Syrian support to ASALA, if such does indeed exist, would become understandable. Compared to most countries, Syria is relatively unconcerned about its connections with terror groups. But here again it should be stressed that reports of Syrian logistics support to ASALA have never received official confirmation. In any case, in light of the copious evidence about ASALA activities on Syrian soil, Turkey has put pressure on Syria, and in October 1983 it was reported that the Armenian activists had been deported from the Lebanese Beka'a Valley.[107] However, this report, apparently of Syria origin, was almost certainly for external consumption only, and it did not refer to any steps aimed at curbing organized Armenian activity on Syrian territory. Hence it may safely be assumed that such activity will continue, both inside and emanating from Syrian territory, even at the expense of tension with Turkey.

ASALA activists also arrived in Iran, apparently after the evacuation of Beirut in the summer of 1982. Toward the end of 1983 tentative connections were reported to have been established between officials close to the Iranian government and ASALA members: during a meeting (no precise date is known) in Teheran between the organization's representatives who had arrived from Beirut and Europe, and a number of Iranian clerics, a discussion took place on ways to assist ASALA with funds, arms and training.[108]

In August 1983 it was reported that ASALA members, together with Iraqi and Kurdish exiles, had joined in an Iranian attack on Iraqi territory at the key position of Hajj Umran.[109] Moreover, Iran and Syria are united in their hostility to France, due to the latter's foreign policy, specifically the support it extends to Iraq in the war with Iran, its involvement in Lebanon, and the asylum France has extended to Iranian exiles. During July and August 1983, ASALA initiated a spate of bombings in Teheran against various French representations, in addition to which telephone threats in the name of ASALA were issued from there. Under prevailing conditions in Iran, such activities would seem impossible without at least the tacit consent of the regime. Otherwise, the risks for ASALA would simply have been too great.

And indeed, events since the beginning of 1984 point to the possibility that ASALA is not as free to operate in Teheran as it would appear. Two out of five attempted strikes at Turkish diplomats during March 1984 were frustrated due to government intervention, and a number of Armenian terrorists were arrested. During an earlier interview, in October 1983, one of ASALA's leaders denied the existence of relations between Iran and ASALA by saying that dozens of ASALA members were imprisoned in Iran, and that two of its members had been executed on order of the authorities in 1981. To this he added the seemingly ambiguous contention that "everything that is being said about cooperation between us and the Iranian government is intended to harm the regime indirectly, by spreading rumors, instead of confronting the regime directly."[110]

In the course of its efforts to marshal new sources of support following the evacuation of Beirut, the organization has apparently also turned to Libya.[111] In view of Libyan leader Qadhafi's declared policies in support of terrorist organizations, it is by no means impossible that ASALA's aid requests have received a positive answer. Neither is there reason to suppose that Libya would hesitate to use ASALA's good services in order to irritate France, whose foreign policies are often directly opposed to Libyan interests, particularly in Africa. But there has been no open expression of this tendency up to now.

In this connection, it was reported that Vicken Tcharkutian, one of the suspects in connection with a bomb attack on Canadian airline offices in Los Angeles (May 30, 1982), fled to Libya after French authorities had released him, following his initial arrest when his plane landed in France, and that he was later following an advanced terrorist training course there.[112]

In addition to the countries already mentioned, ASALA was reported to be regrouping in the Greek sector of Cyprus immediately following the evacuation of the terrorists from Beirut in September 1982. This reorganization, even if it was never officially acknowledged, was probably accompanied by far more active support than mere connivance. As far back as October 1981, ASALA announced that it maintained connections with leftist Cypriot organizations.[113] Backing for ASALA activities on the island apparently originated with the highest quarters in the local government, which owed its stability to the local communist party. According to one report from 1982, the interior and defense ministers of the Greek-Cypriot government were instructed to withdraw all police supervision from the local Armenians; the deputy commissioner of police was transferred to another position because he disregarded these instructions.[114] According to the same source, Greek security agents passed on documents and passports to Armenian terrorist activists. Similar passports reportedly were supplied to the activists who murdered a Turkish diplomat in Belgrade on March 6, 1983, an assassination carried out by the JCAG.[115]

According to one source, the Armenian National Committee regularly convenes in Athens.[116] The nature of this body's connections with ASALA is not clear. According to yet another source, ASALA has offices in Athens, operating under the name "The Cyprus Armenian Greece Organization."[117] It is possible that beyond a basic similarity of ideas, this body does not actually serve ASALA's interests.

Turkey has for years attacked the Greek and Cypriot governments for actively supporting Armenian terror directed against the country. Even if available facts are insufficient to prove these accusations conclusively, those that refer to heightened Armenian political activity in these two countries would appear to be justified. At any rate, while the Greek and Greek-Cypriot governments may not actively support Armenian activity in general, and that of ASALA in particular, it is clear that it is carried out with at least their tacit consent.

In conclusion, available evidence seems to show that ASALA maintains connections with a number of states. The most credible reports refer to an actual organizational infrastructure — particularly in Syria. From ASALA's standpoint, these relationships, apart from a political identity of views, are founded on pragmatic considerations, arising from the fact that ASALA was forced to abandon its strongholds in Beirut. At the same time, it does not appear as if the physical proximity of Iran and Syria to Turkey is a significant factor in this redeployment. ASALA is at present not in a position to operate within Turkey itself, and it is doubtful whether it has the capacity to plan for such an option within the foreseeable future.

ASALA did not come to Syria, or possibly even to Iran, as an integrated organization. Certain extremist elements headed for

Syria following the split in the organization after the evacuation of Beirut, while the more moderate elements transferred their activities to Europe. ASALA's relations with countries such as Iran and Syria strengthen assumptions about a radicalization and escalation of its activities, but at the same time they call into question the degree of independence ASALA's future activities will enjoy.

VI. Asala and the International Armenian Community

The Armenian communities in the East and the West have always been inclined toward identification with, and loyalty to the environment or country in which they resided, and as such they have adapted themselves to the characteristic way of life of their surroundings. This tendency has provided the exile community with a feeling of permanence and continuity, opening the way to the assimilation of Armenians in all aspects of life in their new places of residence. Clearly this accommodation had a price in the form of a certain loss of roots. One result is that many youngsters of Armenian origin (particularly in the West) are today unable to speak the Armenian language. In contrast, there are other Armenian communities which remain faithful to their Armenian cultural and religious heritage, and where the youngsters are being nurtured on stories about the tragedies which have struck their nation in the course of the generations. The most vivid and traumatic memories are of course connected with the events of 1915, about which in many cases they would have heard from people who witnessed them at first hand.

The appearance of ASALA in 1975 signified a radical departure from the approach which had characterized the Armenian struggle for international recognition during the preceding fifty years. Until that year quiet political activity had been conducted by the old-established Armenian political parties — the Hunshak and Dashnak — which were founded back at the end of the 19th century. But these parties failed to serve as a unifying factor for the Armenian community, despite the absence of any inspirational alternative except the integration of the Armenians in their countries of exile — not to mention the fact that they never for one moment ceased their traditional rivalries. Thus one reason for ASALA's establishment among the younger generation was an accumulation of frustration concerning the absence of progress in the political processes. To this disappointment must be added the inspiration provided by the revolutionary, militant nationalist forces holding sway in Beirut during the mid-1970s. Despite this focus on the past, there clearly existed within the international Armenian community a nationalistic undercurrent, as shown by the relatively short time — less than a year — it took the Dashnak

Party to establish the Justice Commando for the Armenian Genocide (JCAG) organization, after recognizing the challenge ASALA was posing to the established rightist Armenian bodies.

Then as now, both organizations have recruited their members from among the younger generation of Armenians, with the difference that the JCAG looks toward the Armenian community in the United States, whereas ASALA has sought its support among the Armenian population of Beirut, the city in which it was established (this, in turn, would seem to be a result of the totally different atmospheres within the two communities). In addition, it would appear as if the tensions between ASALA and the general Armenian community are far more pronounced than those between this community and the JCAG. This means, for instance, that ASALA is forced to take recourse to extreme measures, such as extortion, to extract money from the community,[118] quite unlike the JCAG. When in January 1982 a member of the latter organization was arrested in Los Angeles for the murder of a Turkish diplomat, he was released on bail thanks to a multitude of small, voluntary donations collected among the local Armenian community. These differences in support are partly a consequence of ASALA's leftist ideological basis, which is alien to the majority of Armenians throughout the world. The historical injustice they suffered is of course understood within a nationalist context, but this does not imply an interpretation in the sense of "national liberation" within the framework of an international revolution, which is the way many nationalistic groups throughout the world express this concept today. And of course many Armenians recognize that the Soviet Union is no less responsible for the demise of the independent Armenian Republic than are Turkey and the West.

The rivalry between ASALA and the JCAG has found expression in manifestos in which the two organizations attack each other. Following the bomb attack at Orly Airport on July 15, 1983, a spokesman of the Dashnak Party, Henry Papazian, gave details about ASALA in a press conference, and claimed that the organization was being manipulated by a "foreign government" in order to create unrest in France.[119]

Even so, it is through acts of terror — even if they have caused public protests and opposition — that the Armenian issue has been brought to the attention of world public opinion. On July 22, 1983, the 11th session of the Armenian National Congress opened in Lausanne to an unprecedented public response. This body, which succeeded in rallying 200 delegates representing Armenians from all over the world, was intended to serve as a platform for the "silent majority" among the exiles. The Congress' program favors a diplomatic approach. However, with the exception of the leftist revolutionary motive, its aims are to a large extent identical to those of ASALA: it demands international recognition of the Armenian genocide of 1915, the formal recognition of the Congress by the United Nations, and the establishment of an independent Armenian state, to include Soviet Armenia.[120] This time Lausanne was selected as the site of the Congress, because it was in this town that, exactly 60 years previously, the international agreements were signed dividing Armenia between Turkey and the Soviet Union, thus putting an end to the independent Armenian republic. The purpose of the meeting was to set up a preparatory committee to lay the foundations for a permanent, world-wide organization, in which the organizers looked to both the World Zionist Organization and the Palestine National Council as their model.[121]

The organizer of the Congress was James Karnousian, an Armenian priest residing in Switzerland. Karnousian claimed that he objected to violence, but found himself unable to oppose it unconditionally. Although he denounced the ASALA attack at Orly Airport, which (no doubt intentionally) took place one week before the opening of the assembly in Lausanne, he added that it was thanks to terrorism that the Armenian issue had received international attention.[122] The Armenian National Congress serves as a rallying point for Armenian groups not associated with ASALA, but from time to time voices can be heard from its midst too, calling for selective terror. Evidently these groups feel a sense of obligation to Armenian terrorist activity, and this is their way of acknowledging it. Even so, activities such as those of the Congress might pose a problem for ASALA, presenting, as they do, an alternative to both terrorist activity, and to the conservative forces within the Armenian community which so far have only proved their inability to advance the Armenian national cause. Evidence to this effect may be found in the frictions between ASALA and the National Armenian Movement in France, and its leader, Jean-Marc Toranian. In March and October 1983, two attempts were made on Toranian's life in Paris: the first failed due to a technical mishap; in the second, Toranian was slightly wounded. Toranian himself accused ASALA of trying to punish him for the alienation of his movement from ASALA's radical tendencies.[123]

VII. Western States' Attitudes Toward Armenian Terrorism

Europe has been the principal scene of ASALA's activities since the day of its foundation. In more recent years the organization has shifted part of its activities to Canada and the United States, countries which were mainly the domain of the JCAG.

Armenian terrorist activity presents the western states with several complex problems in terms of their reaction. These are typical of the dilemmas which face any state confronted with political terror, particularly when carried out by foreign organizations. An iron fist policy on the part of the countries concerned — arrests of terrorists found on their territory, deportation of suspects, or the meting out of heavy prison sentences aimed at deterring terrorists from abusing their territorial integrity — is liable to produce open confrontation, and turn the country into a direct target of the terrorist organization rather than an incidental victim. A policy of ignoring terrorist activity, on the other hand, is liable to raise uneasy questions — both inside the country and abroad — about its ambivalent attitude and lack of consistency with regard to political terror. This applies particularly when a country which is accustomed to reacting harshly against internal terror, suddenly shows leniency, or even disregards the activities of a foreign organization operating within its territory. With regard to Armenian terrorism, such a casual attitude could be interpreted as passive support for the objectives of this struggle. Indeed, such tacit identification might affect relations between the western countries and Turkey, the principal target of the struggle, which also happens to be one of the important members of NATO. Moreover, the experience of a number of countries has taught that even turning a blind eye toward the establishment of a terrorist infrastructure on their soil provides no immunity against attack.

These and other considerations determine the reactions of the western states toward Armenian terrorism. There is no uniformity in these reactions, and the practical behavior of a given country may vary according to circumstances, and to the weight and potential repercussions of the problem. Thus the actions of the western states in countering Armenian terrorism are characterized by a lack of consistency. On the one hand, terrorists are arrested and jailed, but at the same time there is a tendency to avoid imposing harsh sentences, and often suspects are released within a short time — if not immediately. In addition, attempts are made by some countries to negotiate with ASALA, in order to try to ensure that it will not operate on their soil. Turkish sources have claimed time and again that ASALA has concluded agreements with several European countries, under which they will tolerate terrorist actions on their soil, provided that no local targets are hit. Switzerland, France, and Italy have been mentioned in this regard.[124]

Switzerland is sympathetic to the Armenian cause and, as mentioned before, hosted the 11th meeting of the Armenian National Congress. Turkish accusations notwithstanding, there is no evidence that the Swiss government has ever tried to come to terms with ASALA. Even so the organization has proved that it is able to exert pressure on the Swiss authorities, as shown by the speedy release of two ASALA members who were arrested in Geneva on October 3, 1980, following a spate of attacks on Swiss targets by ASALA, using the code name "3rd of October Movement." During the following year, a series of attacks were launched against Swiss targets under the pseudonyms "9th of June Organization" — in commemoration of the date (June 9, 1981) on which a member of the organization was arrested in Geneva — and "Swiss 15 Group," so called because of the 15-year jail sentence imposed on the same man on December 19, 1981. This heavy sentence no doubt signified a hardening of Swiss policy against Armenian terror. Since 1982 there has been a noticeable falling off in ASALA activity against Switzerland, and after 1983 not a single attack was recorded. Even so, three of the organization's members are still in Swiss jails today, which makes it doubtful whether ASALA's present restraint with regard to this country will endure.

Italy. During the years 1979-80 ASALA operated three times on Italian soil, in conjunction with a series of bomb attacks against western airline offices. In addition, the Alitalia office in Madrid was the object of an attack in 1980, and in 1981 the Alitalia offices in Paris were bombed. Since then no attacks by ASALA against Italian targets have been recorded. The last incident was unusual, as ASALA had by this time stopped attacking western targets, unless for a direct reason. Even so it was reported in February 1982 that a "truce" had been arranged between ASALA and Italy through PLO mediation. According to this agreement, the existence of which has not been confirmed by any other source, the organization undertook to refrain from actions against Italian targets. The negotiations, said to have been conducted through intermediaries, took place in Beirut at the end of 1981 during the visit of a delegation of the Italian intelligence service, which also included members of the Christian Democratic Party. The same source adds that Hagop Hagopian later declared the agreement null and void, since the Italians had failed to keep their end of the bargain.[125] There are some questions about the reliability of the information, in view of the fact that not a single instance is known of what could be construed as a breach of promise, e.g., an arrest of ASALA operatives by the Italians. Apart from this it seems logical that if anything of the kind had indeed occurred, the organization would have retaliated, as it did earlier against France and Switzerland — and nothing of this kind happened either.

France. The relationship between France and Armenian terrorism is rather more complex. The present Armenian community in France consists of some quarter of a million people, and several legal political organizations are active among them. The atmosphere in France has always been sympathetic to the Armenian nation, with understanding expressed for the frustrations in its history due to the lack of international recognition. This, in addition to the traditionally liberal French attitude toward everything concerned with exiles and those persecuted because of their political views. Thus, various French government officials have in recent years voiced their sympathy with the Armenians' struggle for recognition of their rights, while blaming Turkey for its categorical refusal to accept responsibility for the 1915 massacres. One of the outstanding proponents of this attitude, both in his private views and his official responsibility for France's internal affairs, was French Interior Minister Gaston Deferre.[126]

On April 29, 1984, a statue was unveiled in Paris in commemoration of the Armenian holocaust. On this occasion, Secretary of State for Public Security Joseph Francesci accused Turkey of "obliterating the historical reality of Armenia" by its refusal to accept responsibility for the events of World War I. His statement created tension between France and Turkey, as well as general controversy, and only a few days later a bomb exploded in the immediate vicinity of the new memorial.[127]

The sentences imposed on Armenian terrorists in France have on the whole been relatively light. At the beginning of 1982 four ASALA members, who had been arrested in France following an attack on the Turkish Consulate in Paris (September 24, 1981), were granted the status of political prisoners. This achievement came after they had declared a hunger strike, and as a result ASALA decided to declare an armistice on French soil.[128] At the beginning of 1984 — after the French attitude toward ASALA had hardened — the four were charged with murder and attempted murder, and sentenced to seven years imprisonment, during a trial in which the defense's main effort was directed at proving the historical justification of their acts in light of the events of 1915.[129]

Evidence exists of negotiation attempts between the government of President Mitterand and ASALA. The French government is said to have tried to use its connections with the PLO to conclude a mutual "non-aggression treaty" with ASALA. According to the same source, former French prime minister Pierre Mauroy was personally involved in these negotiations.[130] The French newspaper *Liberation* wrote that PLO official Abu Iyad mediated between ASALA and the French government, by passing on its demands to Joseph Francesci during a secret meeting between the two.[131] Other reports have been confirmed by ASALA: Mihran Mihranian (probably identical with Hagop Hagopian) criticized France for not living up to its agreement not to detain organization members when Vicken Tcharkutian — who was wanted by the American authorities — was arrested on June 4, 1982, when his plane landed on French soil.[132] As already mentioned, the man was released shortly afterwards, out of fear of revenge by ASALA; he continued to Cyprus, and from there apparently to Libya.[133]

Since the arrest of Monte Melkonian at Orly Airport in November 1981, ASALA has claimed responsibility for dozens of bomb attacks on French targets under the code name "Orly Group." The group's activities against French targets continued until the end of 1984. Since mid-1983 these actions have been explained with reference to a number of arrests carried out by the French government within the Armenian community in Paris, following the explosion at Orly Airport on July 13, 1983. Hagop Hagopian was spotted in Paris as early as February 1983, and it now seems that his arrival was connected with the planning of the explosion. At the time the French police refrained from arresting him, and merely kept him under surveillance, presumably in order to avoid aggravating relations with ASALA. But following the blast, some

50 Armenian activists were arrested: twelve were deported from France (which refused a Turkish request for extradition), and another twelve were charged with terrorist activity, and were still under arrest at the end of 1984.[134] These large-scale arrests show that the French government, having been convinced that looking the other way was ineffective, decided to harden its attitude toward ASALA. The possibility cannot be excluded that, as a result of this mailed fist policy, ASALA may intensify its activity against this country in the future.

The *United States* has so far never hesitated to arrest and sentence Armenian terrorists following attempts or attacks with which they were connected. As far as is known, seven JCAG members are jailed in the United States. To date this organization has done nothing to secure their release, no doubt due to its wish to avoid a direct clash with US authorities, beyond its traditional activity of attacking Turkish targets even on American soil. On May 30, 1982, four ASALA members were arrested in Los Angeles following an attempt to attack the Air Canada offices at the local airport. This attempt took place a short time after Canada had arrested four ASALA members on a charge of extorting money from Armenian businessmen in Toronto. This incident, too, has so far not led to attacks by ASALA against American targets, possibly out of a desire to avoid alienating its few existing sources of support among the local Armenian community.

The United States took an official stand with regard to the Armenian issue in 1975, when the Congress adopted a resolution to declare April 24 of that year the "Day of Remembrance of Man's inhumanity to Man:"

> The President of the United States is authorized and re-
> quested to issue a proclamation calling upon the people of
> the United States to observe such day as a Day of Remem-
> brance for the victims of genocide, especially those of
> Armenian ancestry, who succumbed to the genocide
> perpetrated in 1915....[135]

Notwithstanding this sentiment, a State Department spokesman noted not long ago that friendship toward the Armenians was not considered worth the loss of US friendship with Turkey.[136]

The insistence on maintaining close ties with Turkey forms an integral part of the western attitude toward the Armenian question, and certainly overrides considerations of internal security. Still, the fact that no Armenian terrorist has ever been extradited to Turkey (there are today some 25 ASALA members jailed in the United Kingdom, Holland, France, the United States, Canada, Sweden, and Switzerland), seems to show that these countries prefer to contend with the problem within their own, internal framework, whatever difficulties might ensue.

VIII. Turkey's Reaction to Armenian Terrorism

During the difficult times Turkey experienced following World War I the authorities did not consider denying what is today called "the Armenian question." Apart from Turkey's de jure recognition of the Armenian Republic, the Trial of the Unionists in 1919 could also be construed as an admission of responsibility for the Armenian massacre. But ever since this time, a process of disclaiming this historical injustice has formed one of the cornerstones of Turkish policy. Despite the fact that present-day Turkey is no longer under the same regime as that which determined its policies with regard to the Armenian nation in 1915, the official Turkish position is one of categorical denial, not only of any Turkish responsibility for the slaughter, but even of the fact that such a slaughter took place: "Since there was no genocide, Turks cannot accept something which did not happen, as well as claims pertaining to indemnification for a purposely created myth."[137] Turkey makes vigorous efforts on the diplomatic front to prevent any expressions of sympathy with the Armenian issue on the part of countries or public groups in the world at large. These efforts are accompanied by an intensive propaganda campaign, aimed both at creating a historical record of humanistic behavior by the authorities toward the evacuees of 1915, and rewriting the data concerning the number of victims, which appears so low as to bear no comparison with those published in the course of the years.

Turkish pressure to prevent international recognition of the Armenian holocaust reached a climax during the preparation of a United Nations Human Rights Commission report on the prevention of genocide. In 1973 the committee submitted its draft report to the "Sub-committee on the Struggle against Discriminatory Measures and for the Protection of Minorities," paragraph 30 of which mentioned the Armenian holocaust as the first holocaust during the 20th century. In 1974 this controversial paragraph was deleted, and it was still missing from the final text of the report placed before the UN Committee in 1979. The deletion was carried out despite the objections of the Soviet Union, France, the United States, Austria, Australia and other countries.[138]

Turkey considers the present-day Armenian struggle, whether by violent or political means, to be devoid of any valid historical justification, and directed by foreign powers interested in destabilizing Turkey. In this context, the same accusations are repeated that were already leveled against the Armenians during World War I:

> In fact, a thorough study of history reveals that for the last hundred years Armenians have served to alien interests [sic] in return of some promises of others, but they could not achieve anything when those foreign interests were realized. Again, today the issues in question are related to alien interests. Therefore, it would be appropriate to ask how long the Armenians would continue to serve as a tool in the hands of another power....[139]

As for Turkish hostility toward Syria because of the latter's support for ASALA, Ankara has applied diplomatic pressure regarding ASALA bases on Syrian territory. Indeed, tension between the two countries due to ASALA reached such heights in 1983 that in the fall of that year ASALA was cited as the reason why Turkey had built two dams to block the waters of the Euphrates which flow into Syrian territory, as a result of which power shortages were caused in Syria.[140]

There have also been rumors about the Turks organizing a liquidation campaign of ASALA members. In December 1982, three Armenian militants were reportedly assassinated in Athens, Beirut, and the Netherlands; according to ASALA the three were murdered by Turkish agents.[141] There is no confirmation of this report from any other source. In June 1983 Turkish government sources announced that an operation by the Turkish army against Kurds along the Iraqi border was in fact also directed against Armenian activists.[142] Still later, in October 1983, Turkish agents were rumored to have attacked ASALA activists in the Lebanese Beka'a.[143] While there is no official confirmation of this report, it appears plausible in the light of other evidence detailed above.

This Turkish government policy of countering Armenian terror is apparently new. As mentioned above, Turkey's main countermeasure throughout the years has consisted of accusing other states of supporting the Armenian position, or even "directing" the organization itself. All this has been accompanied by consistent denials of any share, or involvement, in the tragic history of the Armenian people.

IX. Conclusion

Irrational Terror or Political Instrument?

In the course of the last few years Armenian terrorist activity has become a source of concern to those circles and countries which — potentially or in practice — form the key targets for its attacks. At the same time the Armenian question, and the nationalistic claims arising from it, have gained widespread public interest. The question that occupies us here concerns the relationship, if any, between Armenian terror and the declared aims of the struggle. In other words, how rational is the use of terror as a means of resolving the Armenian problem?

The first objective of ASALA and of the other Armenian terrorist organizations (e.g., the JCAG) was to bring the Armenian issue to the attention of the international community, and to achieve recognition of the 1915 massacre.

Political terror is a weapon in the hands of organizations which are unable, or unwilling, to satisfy themselves with non-violent political measures to achieve their aims. ASALA spokesmen have time and again emphasized that their recourse to terror was a direct result of continued international indifference, and a conspiracy of silence concerning everything connected with the injustice inflicted on the Armenian nation. Even spokesmen of Armenian political bodies, such as the Armenian National Congress, have expressed themselves in the same vein. In terms of the awareness of international public opinion, then, the recourse to terrorist activity was bound to succeed. But as regards Armenian political or militant groups' demands for official recognition of the 1915 massacre, the situation is far more complex.

World War II resulted in a greater sensitivity within the world community to the systematic, large-scale murder of national groups. On December 9, 1948, the United Nations General Assembly adopted the "Convention on the Prevention and Elimination of the Crime of Genocide," which defined genocide as "Acts committed with the intent to destroy, in whole or in part, a national ethnical, racial, or religious group...." But it takes more than generally ·worded declarations to accuse a specific country of genocide. The moment one wants to place the blame, other considerations come into play that are entirely unrelated to the issue of international morality — and in the specific case of

Turkey, considerations are dominated by this country's place in the western community and its importance as a NATO partner. The world Armenian community in general, and ASALA in particular, possess no political means of their own to exercise pressure. International political considerations also determine the tenor of the reporting of incidents with which terrorist organizations are connected: if the western press mentions the Armenian holocaust at all, the reports are usually careful to maintain a neutral stance, and avoid attaching any blame to Turkey, or to the political processes that resulted in the annexation of historic Armenia by the Soviet Union and Turkey.

Another central objective of ASALA's struggle — unlike the goals of other Armenian political movements or militant groups — is to regain the independence of the Armenian nation on its historic soil. This target would seem even more irrational and unattainable than that of gaining international recognition.

The Armenians themselves tend to identify with the Zionist movement, and the establishment of the State of Israel is seen by them as the ultimate model for their own nationalist aspirations.[144] Even the Armenian National Congress held in Lausanne in July 1983 was described by its organizers as an attempt to establish a body similar to the World Zionist Congress (as well as, paradoxically, the Palestine National Council, since the organizers consider the way in which the Palestinian nationalist struggle is being conducted as a prototype of the kind of struggle which could help them to realize their vision). There are indeed certain parallels between the fate of the Jewish people and that of the Armenians: both were turned into nations of refugees during a certain stage of their history, and both have been subjected to systematic attempts of extermination. But the establishment of the State of Israel, apart from the nationalist Zionist struggle against the British Mandate and the Arab states, was made possible by the preparedness of the world community to support the establishment of a Jewish national home, at a moment when the impressions left by World War II were still fresh in the mind of nations worldwide. The Armenian people may have had a similar opportunity following World War I, but due to internal as well as external causes it failed to grasp it and translate it into reality. The cruelest comparison of all was drawn by Hitler, on the even of World War II when, talking about the Jewish problem, and in order to prove the indifference of the international community, he asked rhetorically: "Who talks today of the Armenians?"

Turkey itself has for years strenuously and consistently denied any liability to the Armenian people, and it seems unwilling to recognize either Armenian rights of any kind, or, for that matter, any obligation to pay compensation. There does not exist today a single international actor capable, or for that matter interested, in inducing Turkey to agree to the return of large numbers of Armenians, or to relinquish its part of Armenia for the benefit of an Armenian group or a foreign state. In any case, any change in Turkey's regional status, or its sovereignty over any part of its present territory, would cause violent upheavals in the balance of power between the existing blocs, in which the issue of the historic Armenian territories would play but a marginal role.

Global considerations aside, there exists the Armenian question on the internal, Turkish level. The eastern Anatolian regions are today densely populated with Kurds — traditional enemies of the Armenians — who present serious minority problems in all their countries of residence: Syria, Iraq, Iran, and of course Turkey itself. In the summer of 1983 the dissident faction of ASALA issued a call to concentrate on a popular struggle within Turkey, in concert with anti-government forces among the Kurds; no doubt a similar possibility has been considered within leading circles of ASALA itself. But beyond the question of turning Turkish Armenia into a base for armed struggle, a possibility which under present circumstances would hardly appear feasible, the Kurds and the Armenians themselves appear incapable of overcoming their traditional enmity, at least sufficiently to undertake a joint struggle for mutually exclusive objectives.

Nor does the present world-Armenian community evidence any real desire for a return to Armenia. Even the participants in the Armenian National Congress admitted that the idea of an independent Armenia was unrealistic.[145] The overwhelming majority of Armenians in the world today would be satisfied with international recognition of the 1915 holocaust, while accepting the fact that the conditions which at one time enabled the birth of the Armenian Republic are gone, never to return.

One explanation for ASALA that is framed in the kind of rational terms acceptable to Turkey, sees the organization as a tool in the service of the Soviet Bloc. This argument, however, lacks credibility, for although such a connection might be embraced at the leading level of the organization, it is unlikely to be endorsed by

ASALA's rank and file. Apart from this, there has never been any indication of a Soviet connection constituting a central factor in ASALA's international relations.

All this leads us to ask, what *does* motivate the leaders and membership of ASALA to its extremist posture? Is ASALA an aberration in the terrorist landscape, consisting of violent bands fighting to achieve essentially unrealistic objectives? Not necessarily, we believe. For as long as one of the objectives is to break the silence around the subject, the declared strategy of the organization offers a legitimizing framework for activists seeking a way of expressing themselves. The very activity creates a taste for more, however varied may be the reasons for the participation of those involved. Therefore, the fact that ASALA's ultimate goals may appear unrealistic, does not necessarily point to an underlying collective irrationality, as long as a number of people prove ready and willing to resort to violence at considerable risk to themselves.

Armenian terror is the extreme and violent expression of a state of mind within a community that has never relinquished either its national character or its sense of an internal tension resulting from the injustice inflicted upon it. Even so, the fact that this expression has taken a violent form is not a direct consequence of this frustration. For years, Armenian communities around the world tended to unite around conservative political and religious organizations; the nationalistic fighting spirit was dormant. It took a drastic change in atmosphere, plus a dominant model that could be copied, for Armenian terrorism to blossom. ASALA originated with a group of Armenian youth in Beirut who had fallen under the influence of the militant revolutionary atmosphere created by the Palestinian struggle and the Lebanese civil war during the mid-1970s. Insofar as these youngsters were looking for an outlet into which to channel their militant spirit, they found it in the sad legacy of their nation in which they had been nurtured. Even the JCAG is an expression of the feelings of Armenian youth suffused with a spirit of nationalism and revenge (but without ASALA's leftist ideological signature), although its foundation was more a reaction to the establishment of ASALA, and the power struggle within the Armenian community, than the result of a pragmatic decision on a new *modus operandi*.

The Armenian terrorist organizations, and ASALA in particular, in fact endanger the sympathy which is felt in the West for the

Armenians. A real danger exists that the violence exhibited in recent years by Armenian organizations, coupled with the 1982-83 escalation in ASALA's activities, and its tendency toward non-selective terror, will result in the association of the Armenians in world public opinion with irrational terrorism, no less threatening to the western states than to Turkey. This, in turn, may cause an erosion of the understanding for the reasons behind the phenomenon.

Current Trends

The summer of 1982 marked a significant change in the trends that, during previous years, characterized the Armenian terrorist struggle. Overall, the activity of both ASALA and the JCAG, the two main Armenian terrorist organizations, abruptly declined, due to a combination of external and internal factors.

ASALA is dominated by a small group of militant youth, who are generations removed from the trauma of their people. Even among themselves there are probably some who consider the ultimate goals of the struggle far-fetched and unrealistic, and this prompts them to link the Armenian struggle to some other ideological platform that will justify continuation of their activity. We have noted that ASALA tends to view the Armenian question within the context of the international revolutionary struggle, and that it has become dependent on countries and organizations with a kindred political outlook. Such connections with organizations that are larger and stronger than ASALA itself have from the outset been a necessity, and as such they explain the — possibly inevitable — ideological coloring of the organization, from which, in turn, follows the selection of its targets and primary areas of operation.

ASALA's activities during the early 1980s showed that it was steadily veering away from the declared objectives of the Armenian struggle. Alongside continued attacks on Turkish targets, the majority of the organization's actions were directed against western countries' representatives and interests. The immediate reason for this has been the struggle waged by these countries against Armenian terrorist acts on their territory. This tendency toward confrontation with western states has resulted in a growing alienation between ASALA, and the mainstream of the Armenian national movement. It has also led to schism within the organization itself.

This polarization of opinion was enhanced by the urgent need to reassess present and future objectives that ASALA encountered following the evacuation of its base in Beirut. The rapprochement that followed — matching extremist elements of ASALA with Syria and Iran — only strengthened previous assumptions regarding radical trends among the ranks of the organization. At the same time, ASALA's relations with terrorism-sponsoring states call into question the degree of independence it can enjoy.

By mid-1985, three years after the severe blow that it suffered in Beirut, ASALA had not yet overcome its post-Beirut logistics difficulties. Moreover, steps taken by the French security forces against Armenian activists following the July 15, 1983 bombing attack at Orly Airport, obviously impaired efforts to establish a new European base there. During the ensuing two years ASALA did not operate on European soil.

During those two years, active measures were taken by the US against terrorist activity there — including Armenian terrorism. These steps contributed to a sharp decrease in activity by both ASALA and the JCAG. Indeed, the JCAG actually did not claim responsibility for any attack on a Turkish target from the end of 1983 until mid-1985. In addition to reasons already cited, this decline in JCAG activity might be explained by the change in ASALA's status in the arena of international terrorism as well as within the Armenian community. The emergence of ASALA caused an urgent need for the more conservative streams in the diaspora to fight for recognition in world opinion; once ASALA was weakened, this need must have been reduced.

In fact, credit for attacks against Turkish legations and diplomats after 1983 was claimed (save for a few acts carried out by ASALA in the summer of 1983 and during 1984 in Tehran) by the newborn Armenian Revolutionary Army. This might be a faction that split off from ASALA following a power struggle, but it is more probably a militant element of the JCAG, determined to carry on with the Armenian fight despite the changing conditions and atmosphere. Thus, in mid-1985, after a period of direct confrontation between Armenian extremists and western states, the militant struggle seemed to be moving back toward the more traditionally oriented currents, in the form of the JCAG or its extreme fringes.

For several years in the late 1970s and early 1980s, ASALA appeared to have resorted to an endless cycle of violence that, ultimately, was unlikely to further the interests of the Armenian diaspora. At the same time ASALA created new currents, both political and militant, that took up the struggle. Undeniably, these violent acts have revived the Armenian question, and here lies the main and most striking achievement of the terrorists.

Appendix 1.

Organizations Connected with Armenian Terrorist Activity

A. Armenian organizations which have consistently carried out terrorist activities:

1. *ASALA — Armenian Secret Army for the Liberation of Armenia,* which forms the subject of this research. ASALA frequently avails itself of pseudonyms in order to claim responsibility for attacks or propagandistic messages. The names under which it has appeared so far are:

    — 3rd of October Movement; attacks against Swiss targets.
    — 9th of June Organization; attacks against Swiss targets.
    — Swiss 15 Group; attacks against Swiss targets.
    — Orly Group; attacks against French targets.
    — September France; attacks against French targets.
    — Armenian Red Army; responsibility for the murder of a Turkish diplomat in Rotterdam in July 1982.
    — World Punishment Organization. The connection with Armenian terror in general, and ASALA in particular has not been proven. An organization of this name claimed responsibility for two explosions in Switzerland in May 1982.
    — 28th of May; responsibility for two attacks in 1977 and one in 1978, all three on Turkish territory. This body may have represented an effort by ASALA to transfer part of its activities to Turkey itself.
    — Armenian National Committee. According to a Turkish source, an announcement was published in Beirut in 1981 about the "continuation" of the Committee's activity. The announcement does not state the kind of activity involved, and it is possible that we are dealing here with an Armenian political body connected with ASALA. According to other information the Committee holds regular meetings in Athens, with the permission of the Greek government.

— Armenian Peoples Revolutionary Movement; published a manifesto in Nicosia on August 19, 1982, calling upon Armenians living in Cyprus to join the struggle.

— Cyprus Armenian Greece Organization; operates in Greece, reputedly as a front organization for ASALA.[146] No details on the connection between ASALA and this group are known, and no confirmation from any other source is available.

2. *JCAG — Justice Commando for the Armenian Genocide.* This is the second largest, and second most important among the Armenian terror organizations, and as such merits a separate discussion.

3. *ARA — Armenian Revolutionary Army;* claimed responsibility for the murder of a Turkish diplomat in Brussels on July 14, 1983, an attempt to occupy the residence of the Turkish Consul in Lisbon on July 27, 1983, the murder of a Turkish diplomat in Vienna on June 20, 1984, as well as an attempt on the life of a Turkish diplomat on November 19, 1984, also in Vienna. This is an unknown organization, suspected to have seceded from ASALA in the summer of 1983, during which period the organization passed through a serious internal crisis. However, ARA rhetoric is reminiscent of that of the JCAG, lending support to the supposition that this is a nom de guerre for the latter.[147]

4. *NAR — New Armenian Resistance;* first heard of in 1977, claimed responsibility for seven attacks until its disappearance in 1980.

B. Armenian organizations in the Soviet Union:
There reportedly exist two underground organizations in the Soviet Union that work toward the liberation of Armenia and the establishment of an independent Armenia on its historic territory. The two organizations (whose leaders are imprisoned) are:

1. *NUPA — The National United Party of Armenia;* founded in 1963.

2. *AHHRMG — The Armenian Helsinki Human Rights Minority Group;* founded in 1977.

No further details about either of these two groups are known.

C. Other Armenian groups whose names have been mentioned in the course of the years, and whose affiliation and activities have not been established:

- *VEDO — New Resistance Organization;* based in France.
- *EKO — Armenian Liberation and Freedom;* based in France.
- *GEGE — Young Action Group Armenians/Young Action Group;* based in Beirut.
- *Armenian Underground Army.*
- *The New Armenian Revival.*
- *Avengers of the Massacre of the Armenians.* This name may be a pseudonym of the JCAG, by a slight change of its customary appellation.
- *Armenian Revenge Group.*
- *The Armenian Liberation Front.*
- *The Yonikayan Commandos.*

In addition, a Turkish source[148] reports the following organizations as being to all intents and purposes led by ASALA:

- *The Armenian Justice Commando* (=JCAG?).
- *The Armenian Resistance Organization;* founded in 1977.
- *The Armenian Liberation Army.*
- *The Youth Attack Organization.*

The above claim would seem exaggerated, in particular because of the first name, which is reminiscent of the JCAG. No confirmation from any other source is available. Apart from this, a closer scrutiny of the various names raises doubts whether the multiplicity, if not duplication, of names is not a result of an erroneous translation of the names of the main organizations, or even a deliberate attempt to create an impression of more widely-based activity. Such an impression would serve not only the interests of the Armenian terror groups themselves, but also those of international bodies (and the Turkish government) who seek to emphasize the threat posed by Armenian terror.

Appendix 2.

Incidents by Type of
Target, 1981 through 1984

Until the end of 1979 the Armenians restricted their attacks to Turkish targets around the world. These consisted in particular of airline companies, travel agencies and official legations. In November 1979 ASALA began to attack western targets as well, accompanied by declarations against western imperialism, Zionism, and all other nations maintaining relations with the "fascist" regime in Turkey. This shift was in line with the organization's leftist guiding principles.

The principal justification for ASALA's attacks against western nations consists of the latter's activities against Armenian terror, including the arrest of Armenian terrorists. The principal western targets are Switzerland (against which ASALA operated under the pseudonyms "3rd of October Movement," "9th of June Organization," and "Swiss 15 Group"), and France (under the pseudonyms "Orly Group," and "September France").

The 49 terrorist attacks carried out by ASALA in the course of 1981 were directed against:

French targets	21 attacks
Swiss targets	18 attacks
Turkish targets	8 attacks
Italian targets	1 attack
American targets	1 attack

The 24 terrorist attacks carried out by ASALA in the course of 1982 were directed against:

French targets	8 attacks
Turkish targets	7 attacks
Swiss targets	4 attacks
Canadian targets	3 attacks
Saudi Arabian targets	1 attack

In the same year ASALA published a threat against any nation holding Armenian terrorists as prisoners.

The 22 attacks carried out by ASALA in the course of 1983 were directed against:

French targets	11 attacks
Turkish targets	8 attacks
Swedish targets	1 attack

Another two attacks were directed against an Armenian activist (see note*** in Appendix 3 below).

The 7 attacks carried out by ASALA and other, unidentified, Armenian terrorists during 1984, were directed against:

Turkish targets	6 attacks
French targets	1 attack

In fact, in the course of the entire year 1984, ASALA itself claimed responsibility for only 1 attack, directed against a French target.

Appendix 3.

Incidents by Modus Operandi, 1980 through 1984

note: Diplomatic target = diplomats, consuls, etc.
Other representations = airlines, banks, etc.
Civilian targets = attacks in public places, cinemas, restaurants, etc.

TARGETS	Assassination * ** ***					Threats ****					Explosions					Armed Attacks *****				
	80	81	82	83	84	80	81	82	83	84	80	81	82	83	84	80	81	82	83	84
Turkish																				
Diplomats	3	4	5	1	5						4	1	1	1	1	1	1		2	
Representations											6	1		2					2	
Civilian targets																			1	
Western																				
Diplomats							5	3	2		2	4		3					1	
Representations						1	2		2		14	15	4	2			1	1		
Civilian targets	1						1		1			14	9		1					
Armenian & Arab																				
Diplomats																				
Representations													1							
Civilian targets		2																		
Total attacks/year by type of event	4	4	5	3	5	1	8	3	5	—	26	35	15	8	2	1	2	1	6	—

Total attacks per year — 1980:32; 1981:49; 1982:24; 1983:22; 1984:7.

Explanation of asterisks:

* An exception during the year 1982 was the murder of the Turkish Consul in Burgos in Bulgaria (September 9, 1982). This act seems exceptional in view of ASALA's known connections with the Eastern Bloc. Conceivably ASALA sought to sabotage Turkey's renewed (mainly economic) relations with Bulgaria. The event is included here, although it must be noted that both ASALA and the JCAG claimed responsiblity.

** The total number of assassinations includes the capture of an ASALA activist in London on September 9, 1982. He was arraigned and tried in July 1983 on a charge of planning the assassination of the Turkish ambassador in London.

*** In March and October 1983 two attempts were made in Paris on the life of Jean-Marc Toranian, an Armenian activist. Following the March attempt, Toranian accused ASALA of wanting to harm him because of differences of opinion on the way the Armenian struggle should be conducted.

**** In mid-October 1983 ASALA threatened to blow up the Paris- Marseille express train. An explosion took place on this line on December 31, 1983, responsibility for which was claimed by Carlos.

***** Barricade-hostage incidents are included under the heading Armed Attacks.

The figures in the tables refer to attacks carried out either by ASALA, or by Armenians who are presumed to have acted on behalf of ASALA. Figures do not include attacks for which responsibility was claimed by the JCAG.

Appendix 4.

Incidents by Geographical Distribution, 1981 through 1984

During 1981 Western Europe formed the principal scene of ASALA's activities. The 49 recorded events occurred in the following countries:

France	16	Ten against French targets, three against Turkish targets, one against an American target, one against a Swiss target, and one against an Italian target.
Switzerland	9	Seven against Swiss targets, one against a Turkish target, and one against a French target.
Lebanon	5	Four against French targets, and one against a Turkish target.
Iran	3	Two against Swiss targets, and one against a French target.
Italy	3	Two against Swiss targets, and one against a Turkish target.
Denmark	2	One against a Swiss target, and one against a Turkish target.
United States	2	Both against Swiss targets.
Spain	1	Against a Swiss target.

In addition there were eight cases of threats during the year 1981. Five of these were directed against French representations and other targets — and three of these originated in Beirut. Two threats, by an uncertain source, were directed at Swiss representations; one threat, from an equally unknown source, was directed against the Turkish government.

In 1982 Western Europe also formed the main area of ASALA activity. The 24 known events occurred in the following countries:

France	7	All directed against French targets.
Canada	4	Three against Turkish targets, one against a Canadian target.

Switzerland	4	All against Swiss targets.
United States	1	Against a Canadian target.
Greece	1	Against a Saudi Arabian target.
Netherlands	1	Against a Turkish target.
Turkey	1	Against a Turkish target.
Bulgaria*	1	Against a Turkish target.
England**	1	Against a Turkish target.

*   See note in Appendix 3, 1982 statistics.
** See note** in Appendix 3.

In addition, there were three threats in 1982: one against all western nations that had imprisoned ASALA members, one against the Canadian government, and one against the French government. The source of these threats is unknown.

In 1983 Europe continued to be the main theater of ASALA's activities, but for the first time a relatively large number of attacks took place in Teheran. The total of 22 events occurred in the following countries:

Iran	8	All against French targets.
France	7	Four against Turkish targets, one — a threat — against a French target (see note**** in Appendix 3) and two against an Armenian target (see note*** in Appendix 3).
Luxembourg	1	Against a Turkish target.
Belgium	1	Against a Turkish target.
Greece	1	A threat directed at a French target.
Portugal	1	Against a Turkish target.
Denmark	1	A threat directed at a Swedish target.
West Germany	1	Against a French target.
Lebanon	1	Against a Turkish target.

In 1984 ASALA and/or other unidentified Armenian terrorists carried out seven attacks in:

| Iran | 6 | All against Turkish targets. |
| France | 1 | Against a French target. |

Appendix 5.

Armenian Publications

A large number of publications serve Armenian communities throughout the world. Nothing is known about connections between these publications and ASALA. It is equally unclear to what extent they serve ASALA's political and propaganda objectives. The most important are:

— *ARMENIA:* a publication issued in Beirut — in Arabic, Armenian, and English. There is no information on any issues since September 1982.

— *The Armenian Reporter:* an English-language weekly published in New York, with offices in other cities in the United States. In political terms this is an "independent" publication.

— *Zartonk* ("Awakening"): a publication of the Armenian Youth Attack Organization (see Appendix 1, among the organizations connected with Armenian terrorist actions).

— *Armenian Weekly:* a weekly published in the United States. Apparently reflects rightist circles among the Armenian community, and is connected with the Dashnak Party.

Appendix 6.

Principal Historical Dates

April   — Declared a memorial month by the Armenians in commemoration of the victims of the 1915 massacres.

May 28   — The commemoration of the declaration of the Armenian Republic in 1915.

March 4   — Two Turkish diplomats were assassinated in Paris in the course of a week called by ASALA "Armenian Victory Week."

April 24   — This day has been declared Saints and Martyrs' Day, and as such represents the Armenian memorial day of the 1915 holocaust. On April 24, 1915, the arrests of Armenian intellectuals and leaders began in Istanbul, marking the first step of the expulsions.

Appendix 7. Historical Appendix A

Selected Armenian Documents on the Fate of the Armenians in Turkey

Source: *Armenian Review,* Vol. 37, nos. 1-145 (Spring 1984).
"Documents: The State Department File."
R.G. 59, 867.4016/58

TELEGRAM RECEIVED
From Constantinople
Dated April 27, 1915
Recd. April 28, 10:30 A.M.

Secretary of State,
Washington.
608 April 27, 4 P.M.
Confidential

Over hundred Armenians of better class were arrested ostensibly to prevent revolutionary propaganda. Among the number is Leon Chirinigon a naturalized citizen of Persian origin whose American citizenship is recognized by the Sublime Port. Have taken up matter. Their lives are probably not in danger but they are being deported to the interior. Movement against Armenians forms part of concerted movement against all non-Turkish and non-Union-and-Progress elements and indications exist that it will be followed by action against Zionists. Have also received unfavorable reports about Armenians in interior provinces. Colleagues and I are (#) strong efforts to prevent excesses and stop the movement.

AMERICAN AMBASSADOR CONSTANTINOPLE

(#) Apparent omission.

Copy for Department
AMERICAN CONSULATE
TREBIZOND TURKEY, June 28, 1915

Honorable Henry Morgenthau,
  American Ambassador,
    Constantinople.

Sir:

I have the honor to enclose herewith for the information of the Embassy a copy of the proclamation which has been posted up in public places by the local authorities notifying the Armenians that within five days from its date, namely, on Thursday, July 1st, the entire Armenian population of Trebizond and vicinity including men, women and children will be obliged to turn over to the government such property as they cannot take with them and start for the interior, probably for Eldjezireh or Mosul where they will remain until the end of the war. Upon their return after the war their goods will be returned to them.

It is impossible to convey an idea of the consternation and despair the publication of this proclamation has produced upon the people. I have seen strong, proud, wealthy men weep like children while they told me that they had given their boys and girls to Persian and Turkish neighbors. I know of one Armenian woman who is not in Dr. Crawford's house who has become insane and two other such cases are reported in the same vicinity. Many are providing themselves with poison which they will take in case the order is not rescinded.

At the present time there are no means of transportation available. All horses, wagons and vehicles have been requisitioned for military purposes and the only way for these people to go is on foot, a journey of sixty days or more. At this season of the year in the heat and dust it is simply impossible for women and children and old men to start on such a journey. Even a strong man without the necessary outfit and food would be likely to perish on such a trip.

As I am not permitted to use the cipher code it does not seem best to send an open telegram to the Embassy on this subject, but I have talked with my Austro-Hungarian colleague who has the privilege to use a code and have requested him to express my hearty concurrence with him in urging that some measures be taken at Constantinople to secure a withdrawal of this order if possible or at least a modification so as to spare the old men, women and children from such a journey which would mean their certain destruction.

I called upon the Governor General and asked if some exceptions could not be made and he read to me the enclosed proclamation which he thereupon handed to me saying that he was obliged to follow the text of the proclamation. He assured me however that he had telegraphed to Constantinople asking that an exception be made for Armenians in official positions which I told him I hoped would include the two consular cavasses and clerk who are Armenians.

I enclose a copy of the "Meshveret", dated Sunday, June 27th, which is the official organ of the government published in Trebizond. It contains an article in regard to excesses said to have been committed by Armenians and Greeks upon the family of a Turkish Emam (Priest) at Erganess. Whether it is true or not it is an unfortunate thing to publish here just at this juncture. I have been informed furthermore that there are no Greeks whatever in that section of the country, which would seem to throw doubt upon the whole story.

The people are hopeless but are making preparations to start on the perilous journey. I trust that before the date of departure some modification may be secured.

As there is not time to make translations of the two Turkish enclosures before the mail closes I send them without translations.

I have the honor to be, Sir,
Your obedient servant,
(Signed) OSCAR S. HEIZER
American Consul

Enclosures:
  As stated.

AMERICAN CONSULATE

Trebizond, June 30th, 1915

Honorable Henry Morgenthau
  American Ambassador
    Constantinople.
Sir:—

After mailing my despatch of June 28th to the Embassy further information was received from an eyewitness of the terrible sufferings of the Armenians who were recently expelled from the vicinity of Baibourt and Erezeroum. A Turkish teamster (Mohammedan) who has just returned from Erzerum told a well known Armenian merchant here, with tears in his eyes, of the wretched condition of about 150 Armenian women and children he came upon near Ashkelah in a plain about ten hours from Erzerum. Most of them were nearly naked, all were hungry, many were carrying children. The Turk said he gave them all the money he had to buy bread but realizing his inability to do anything for them of importance and unable to view their sufferings he hurried away.

A gendarme who has recently returned from the region says that the deported people are wandering about in the forests and on the mountains, some of them naked, having been robbed of their honor and of their clothing. Under these circumstances the Armenians of Trebizond, who are aware of the situation there, fully believe that if they are deported from this place they will suffer like treatment on the journey before them. It is probable that they will be sent to Mosul or Eldjezereh although there has been an effort made to have the government change their destination to Gumushhane which is in this vilayet.

The Vali informed that it had been decided to make an exception in favor of old men and women, widows, women expecting to give birth soon, and Armenians in the employment of the Turkish government, but the others would all be sent away.

In the evening of the 28th I advised Dr. Crawford to send an urgent telegram to Mr. Peet regarding the children and teachers in his school, and to request that an effort be made in Constantinople to secure an exception in their favor, to include, if possible, the women and children generally. I offered to send the telegram through the Embassy with the expectation that it would not be stopped and while the information would reach the Embassy first it would not appear to the local authorities here that the consulate was taking too active a part in an affair between the Turkish government and its own subjects.

The Vali has agreed not to molest the Armenian dragoman and two Armenian cavasses of this consulate.

My colleagues the German and Austro-Hungarian Consuls are working hard to secure some modification of the harsh measures, especially in favor of the women and children, by representations here and through their respective Embassies.

I have the honor to be, Sir,
Your obedient servant
Signed: Oscar S. Heizer,
American Consul

AMERICAN EMBASSY
Constantinople

No. 612   November 9, 1915.

The Honorable
   The Secretary of State,
      Washington.

Sir:

I have the honor to enclose herewith a translation of a statement made by Miss Alma Johanson regarding atrocities committed against Armenians in Eastern Anatolia. She is a Swedish lady but has been connected for thirteen years with the German Mission at Moush. Her statement was made in German, the enclosed copy is an English translation of it.

I also herewith enclose a letter from Dr. Post of Konia, together with a translation of a letter (no. 7) received from the Armenian Committee of Dashnaksoutiun.

I shall continue to send you these statements without any comment, as they speak for themselves.

I have the honor to be, Sir,
Your obedient servant,
(Signed) H. MORGENTHAU

Enclosures:
   1/Statement of Miss Johanson;
   2/Dr. Dodd's letter, Oct. 27, 1915;
   3/Report of Dashnaksoutiun, No. 7,
         Oct. 28, 19154. [sic]
      (In duplicate)

Enclosure No. 1
Reports of an eye witness
Miss Alma Johanson (German Missionary)

Towards the end of October when the Turkish war began, the

Turkish Officials started to take everything they needed for the war, from the Armenians. Their goods, their money, all was confiscated. Later on every Turk was free to go to an Armenian shop and take out what he needed or thought he would like to have. Only a tenth perhaps was really for the war, the other was *robbery*. It was necessary to carry food, etc. to the front, at the borders of the Caucasus. In order to carry the necessary burdens, the Government sent out about 300 old Armenian men, many cripples amongst them, and boys not over twelve years old, to carry the goods, which was a three week's journey from Musch to the Russian borders. As every individual Armenian was robbed of everything he ever had, these poor people soon died of hunger and cold on the way. They had on no clothes at all, even these were stolen on the way. If of the 300 Armenian 30-50 returned it was a marvel, the rest were either beaten to death or died for reasons stated above. The winter was most severe in Musch, the gendarmes were sent to raise high taxes and as the Armenians had already given every thing to the Turks, and therefore powerless to pay these enormous taxes, they were beaten to death. The Armenians never defended themselves except when they saw the gendarmes ill-treat their wives and children, and so the result was that the whole village was burnt down merely because a few Armenians tried to protect their families. Toward the middle of April we heard rumors that in Van there were great disturbances. We have heard statements made both from Turks and Armenians, and as these reports agree in every respect it is quite plain there is some truth in them; namely, that the Government of Turkey sent orders that all Armenians were to give up their arms which the Armenians refused to do stating that they require same in case of necessity. This caused a regular massacre. All villages inhabited by Armenians were burnt down. The Turks boasted of having now got rid of all the Armenians. I heard it from the officers myself, their revelling in the knowledge that the Armenians were done away with. Thus the winter passed, things more terrible than one can possibly relate happening every day. We then heard that massacres had started in Bitlis. In Musch everything was being prepared for one, when the Russian arrived at Lice which is about 14-16 hours of Musch, this occupied the attention of the Turks so that the massacre was put off for the time being. Hardly had the Russians left Lice, however, when the whole districts where Armenians dwelt were pillaged and destroyed. This was in the month of May. At the beginning of June, we heard that the whole Armenian population of Bitlis were done away with. It was at this time that we received news that the American Missionary Dr. Knapp was wounded in an Armenian house and that the Turkish Government sent him to Diarbekir. The very first night in Diarbekir he died and the Government explained his death as a result of having *overfed* himself, which of course nobody believes. When there was no one left in Bitlis to massacre their attention was turned to Musch. Up to now cruelties were committed but not too publicly, now they started to shoot people down without any cause, they beat them to death, because they found delight in doing so. In Musch itself, which is a big town, there are alone 25,000 Armenians; around Musch there are 300 villages, every village containing about 500 houses and not one male Armenian and but a few women here and there are visible now. Beginning of July; in the first week of the month 20,000 soldiers came from Constantinople over Harpout to Musch with munition and eleven guns, and besieged Musch. In fact the town was surrounded already since middle of June. At this time the Mutessarif gave orders that we two German missionaries should leave the town and go to Harpout. We pleaded with him to let us stay for we had in our charge all the orphans and patients, but he was angry and threatened to force us away if we did not do as instructed. As we both became sick we were allowed to remain at Musch. I received permission in case we should leave Musch to take the Armenians of our orphanage along but on asking for assurances of safety his only reply was: "You can take them along but being Armenians their heads may and will be cut off on the way." On the 10th of July Musch was bombarded for several hours, they pretended the reason was because some Armenians had tried to escape. I went to see the Mutessarif asking him to protect our houses and his reply was "Serves you right for staying instead of leaving as instructed. The guns are here to put an end to Musch. Take refuge with the Turks." This of course was not possible as we could not leave our charges. A new order was the next day promulgated that the Armenians would be expelled and three days were given them to be ready. They were told to register themselves at the government's office before they left. The families could remain but their property and their money was to be confiscated. The Armenians were unable to go as they had no money to pay the trip and they preferred to die in their houses rather than be separated and endure a lingering death on the road.

As mentioned before three days were given the Armenians to leave but two hours had scarcely elapsed when the soldiers broke into the houses and arrested every one and threw them into prison. The cannons began to fire and thus preventing the people from registering themselves at the government office. We all had to take refuge in the cellar for fear of our orphanage catching fire. It was a heartrending spectacle to hear the cries of the people and children who were being burnt to death in their houses. The soldiers found great delight in hearing these cries and when people who were on the street during the bombardment fell dead the soldiers merely laughed at them. The survivers were sent to Ourfa (nothing but sick women and children). I went to the Mutessarif and begged him to have mercy on the children at least, but in vain, he replied the Armenian children must perish with their nation. All our people were taken from our hospital and orphanage, they left us three female servants. thus Musch was burnt down in this monstrous way. Every officer boasted of the number he had personally massacred thus ridding Turkey of the Armenian race. We left for Harpout; Harpout has become the cemetery of the Armenians, from all directions they have been brought to Harpout to be buried. There they lie and the dogs and the vultures lick their bodies. In Harpout and Mezre the people have had to endure terrible tortures, such as their eye-brows being pulled off, their breasts are cut off, their nails pulled out, their feet are cut off or they hammer nails into them just as they do with horses. This is all done during the night and in order that the people may not hear their screams and know of their agony, soldiers stand around the prisons drumming and blowing whistles. Needless to repeat that many died of these tortures. The soldier then cry "Now let your Christ help you." One old priest was tortured so much into confession that he believing that this pain would cease and he would be left alone cried out in his desperation: "We are revolutionary people." He expected his torture would end now but on the contrary the soldiers said: "What else do we seek for? We have it here from his own lips."And instead of choosing their victims as they did up to the present the officials had all the Armenians, sparing no one, tortured. Beginning of July, 2000 Armenian soldiers were ordered to leave for Aleppo to build roads. The people of Harpout were terrified on hearing this and a panic started in the town. The Vali called the German Missionary, Mr. Eheman, and begged him to quiet the people repeating over and over again that no harm whatsoever would befall these soldiers. Mr. Eheman believed the Vali and quieted the people. But they had scarcely left when we heard that they had all been murdered and thrown in a cave. Just a few managed to escape and we got the reports from them. It was useless to protest to the Vali, the American Consul at Harpout protested several times but the Vali treats him like "air"and in a most shameful manner. A few days later another 2000 Armenian soldiers were despatched via Diarbekir and in order to hinder them from escaping they were left to starve on the way so that they had no power left in them to flee. The Kurds were given notice that the Armenians are on the way and the wives of the Kurds came with their butcher's knives to help the men. In Mezre a public house was erected for the Turks — and all the beautiful Armenian girls and women were put in. At night the Turks were allowed free entrance. The permission for the Protestant and Catholic Armenians to be exempted from deportation arrived only after their deportation. The Government wanted to force the few remaining Armenian to accept the Mohamedan faith. A few did so in order to save their wives and children from the great suffering already witnessed. The people begged us to leave for Constantinople and bring some security for them. On our way to Constantinople we only encountered some old women. No young girls or women were to be seen.

We knew it in November already that there would be a massacre, the Muttesarif of Musch, who was a most intimate friend of Enver Pasha, declared quite openly that they would massacre the Armenians at an opportune moment and exterminate the whole race; before the Russians arrived they intended to first butcher the Armenians and then fight the Russians.

Toward the beginning of April in the presence of a Major Lange and several other high officials, such as American and German Consuls, Ekran Bey said it quite openly, namely their intention to exterminate the Armenian race. All these details plainly show that the massacre was planned.

It is very unsafe now for all Missionaries in the Interior, the officials show their hatred too plainly, and have often told us that they do not see the necessity of our presence.

In a few villages destitute women come begging, naked and sick for alms and protection, we are not allowed to give them anything, we are not allowed to take them in, in fact we are forbidden to do anything for them and they die outside. If permission could be obtained from the authorities to help them? If we cannot endure the sight of these poor people what must it be to them who suffer it themselves.

It is a story written in blood. Two old missionaries and a younger lady (Americans) were sent away from Mardin, treated just like prisoners always in the company of gendarmes, and brought to Sivas. I find such a trip in the present circumstances for the old missionaries a terrible hardship.

★ ★ ★ ★ ★ ★ ★ ★

Enclosure No. 2

October 27, 1915.

Since last writing to you the situation has changed considerably, although the general need and suffering remain. The whole encampment near the railroad has been cleared out and sent on with the exception of some tents belonging to families with contagious cases such as diptheria, scarlet etc. which are being attended to by the belediye physician. There remain however a very large number of people in the city, some say as many as 20,000, who are still permitted to stay here probably through bribes to the police, friends in the Government, etc. Although the above number may be an exaggeration one sees crowds of Armenians everywhere in town and we have the same crowd of about 500 every day to feed and more patients coming to the clinic than we have time to see.

Soon after the great deportation that preceded the arrival of the new Vali, Miss Cushman and I drove out to Kachin Han, the first station of the R.R. towards Eregli, just to follow up the crowd, as a large number had been driven off on foot with the expectation of taking the railroad later on. Kachin Han is about three hours from here by carriage and even so near to Konia as this we found about 100 people, sitting and lying about the Station in utter destitution. They had been there three days; most of them had eaten up all the provisions they had and looked haggard and emaciated, veritable famine victims such as one sees in pictures of an occurring in India. On leaving Konia they had been promised food along the way, and the gendarmes there left saying "geledjek" but the fact that they had had no provision whatsoever made for them. The train from Konia came along while we were there and most of the people dragged themselves to the cars and endeavoured to get on but were pushed back by the gendarmes, partly because they had no tickets and partly because there was no

91

room; so the poor people turned back bitterly and hopelessly to where they had been sitting or lying about the Station. There is a village an hour or two away from the Station and a Turkish baker had driven to the Station for sale but as there was no money to buy the grown people looked at it from the distance, while the little gaunt children drew near to stare at it wistfully. I brought enough to give each person there a loaf and many declared that it was the first food they had had for three days. Some of the people there were intelligent and educated — their sufferings were even greater than those of the villagers who were more accustomed to hardship. There were two women there desperately sick with puny babies tugging away at the breast and getting nothing, their pathetic cries mingled with the groans of the mothers in physical and mental anguish. Among the hundred people there were not half dozen tents and those improvised and of the flimsiest description. All the rest of the people were lying out in the open, day and night, many without even a blanket or quilt. A half mile from the Station I found two old women who were crawling about on hands and knees, too weak to walk; they had been carried off on a wagon ostensibly to go to a village but once out of sight of the gendarmes the driver had dropped them in the field and hurried away. All without exception looked forward to certain death, by starvation nor could we see any other future for them. A few miles further on we found a little heap of clods that had been apparently piled together and then scattered, and near it a bundle of rags full of a child's bones — the skull, with scalp still clinging to it was lying a yard or two away — evidently there had been a hasty burial and the dogs had come and torn the grave to pieces and devoured the body. That same day we found another dead body by the roadside — an old woman wrapped in a torn quilt; also a woman about 40 years old sitting alone by the road, miles away from city or village, with feet bare and swollen, almost pulseless, and evidently crazed from terror and exposure, muttering something about T's who were coming to cut her throat, about her people who had left her behind, and so forth. A little farther on, lying beside an empty wayside stable, we found an old woman, half naked, pulseless, muttering in low delirium and with only a few hours to live. We lifted her into the old stable, covered her with an old quilt that we found near her and drove back to the city, weighed down with the thought of the awful suffering that is going on all over the country, especially to the south-east of us, of which we see such terrible examples at our very doors.

92

Our new executive is affable and pleasant enough but is hand and glove with the clique here and impresses me as insincere. After pushing the deportation vigorously for a few days, things have quieted down again and the Armenians in town are having their hopes revived although we see nothing to ground them upon. The hunger and want in the city are increasing; today we fed over 600. It is blessed work, even if it seems to have no future for the recipients. A lot of the exiles are well qualified to earn a living but the police will not allow them to work.

Next time you write I should be interested to know if the case of Vartuhi, whose sisters from Gumuldjina were abducted, was taken up by the Bulgarian Ministry.

A side light on the rate of the extermination of the Armenians is thrown by a glance at mortality statistics in our hospital which I have been studying lately. In ordinary years the average mortality from all causes is about 4%. This year, among 500 to 600 soldiers we have taken in, it has been about 6%, the increase being doubtless due to the lowered vitality of the soldiers in general. The mortality among Armenians — exiles — who have been admitted to our wards has been over 30% and this in spite of the fact that we have taken in only the ordinary run of maladies and that there has been no epidemic! The nation is being systematically done to death by a cruel and crafty method, and their extermination is only a question of time.

Pray for us as we do for you, and as I am confident we all do that the days may be shortened.

With best wishes,

Faithfully yours,

Wilfred M. Post.

Appendix 8. Historical Appendix B

Selected Turkish Documents on the fate of the Armenians in Turkey

Source: Documents (on Ottoman-Armenians), Vols. I & II,
Turkish Prime Ministry, Directorate-General of
Arms and Information
(from Turkish Military Archives)

DOCUMENT NO: 4

No: 440

Decoded message of 24 August 1330 *(1 September 1914)*
from the Supreme Command in Istanbul.

According to information from the Ambassador in Teheran, the Russians have issued arms to the Armenians in Iran and in Caucasus, Russian Consul in Tabriz has promised Armenians to set up an Armenian state and that the strength of Russian forces around Mako comprises 12,000 infantry, 1200 cavalry and 124 Artillery guns.

Communications exist between Russians and Armenians in Van. The accuracy of this information is not definite. Yet Armenian soldiers must be kept under special conditions and must not be allowed to change their political allegiance.

Arcive No	:	4/3671
Cabin No	:	160
Drawer No	:	5
File No	:	2818
Section No	:	59
Contents No	:	2–10

DOCUMENT NO: 7

To: Command-in-Chief

28.7.330 *(1.10.1914)*

According to information received, the Russians have established guerillas by arming Russian and Turkish Armenians in the

Caucasus and Greeks, and anticipate expanding these guerilla organizations by sending them into Turkish land. These reports are gradually being confirmed, and realised, and Armenian deserters from military units are increasing.

I had submitted the required measures in my letter No: 347 of 10/11 September 1330 (23/24 September 1914). Further measures are required for families of deserters and traitors, to include punishment for villages which shelter and protect the gangs and the dispersing of such villages. These measures should be announced so that everybody will know about them. A definite and general decision is absolutely vital.

Signature

Archive No	:	4/3671
Cabin No	:	160
Drawer No	:	5
File No	:	2811
Section No	:	26
Contents No	:	15-1

DOCUMENT NO: 12

Ministry of Defence
Department of Correspondence
Coding Section

Coded Message from Elazig to the Ministry of Defence

A group of 40-50 Armenian army deserters with arms at Sironik village 2.5 hours from Mus, attacked the Gendarmarie Cavalrymen and police who went to the village to capture them. The clash lasted for two hours. A 200-strong detachment led by Ismail Etendi and the Gendarmarie Commander was dispatched to the scene. Nine of those who resisted were killed. The detachment is still in the village. This is submitted from Acting Commander of Mus division.

8 February 330 (21 February 1915)

Acting Commander 11th Army Corps
Hakki

Archive No	:	1/131
Cabin No	:	101/149
Drawer No	:	14–4
File No	:	2287

Section No   :   32/12
Contents No   :   6–4

DOCUMENT NO: 21

The coded message received from the Mobile Gendarmarie
Command of Van on 16/17 April 1915 (3/4 April 331)

Armenians from Stak District of Van, attacked the gendarmarie troops and stations and cut the telegraph lines.

Detachments have been sent out in requisite directions. The detachment proceeding in the direction of Sitak District has confronted the Armenian bands and engaged in fighting. Presented.

The code is kept at the First Section.

Archive No   :   4–3671
Cabin No   :   160
Drawer No   :   5
File No   :   2818
Section No   :   59
Contents No   :   1–16

DOCUMENT NO: 1911 (107)

NO: 10327

CODED MESSAGE RECEIVED FROM GOVERNOR OF SIVAS, MUAMMER BEY on 9/10.2.331 (22/23 April 1915):

C. 8.2.331 (21 April 1915)

1. The places within the province with a high Armenian population are Karahisar, Susehri, Hafik, Dirigi and Gurun, Gemerek, Amasya, Tokat and Merzifon.

2. To date a great number of prohibited weapons and dynamite have been seized in searches in villages around Susehri, at Tuzhisar and Horasan villages of Hafik and at Ulalas sub-district of the Central region.

3. Armenians have organised and armed a 30,000 strong force from this province, of which 15,000 this way or the other joined the Russian Army while the remaining 15 (thousand) have been assigned with the mission of occupation in the rear, should

our Army, fail to be successful (May God forbid). These have been confirmed with the interrogation statements of the arrested suspects.

4. It has been felt that Armenians are preparing for a rebellion in the Spring, when sheltering is possible in mountains. This has been confirmed by the captured arms and explosives during the Van incident and with the flight of some of the leading figures of the committee.

5. Upon reports that Mirad, a leading Dashnak figure was hiding at Tuzhisar village, I dispatched a contingent. During an armed clash several of the Armenians were killed and about 20 surrendered, the rest escaped. Follow-up operations continue.

6. Upon request from stationed and mobile gendarmerie for support, a strong detachment was sent toward Hafik. Villages expected to take part in the rebellion have been cleared by the military of materials, vehicles and means of attack and defence.

7. The provincial authority has been authorised to invite all men up to 40-50 ages for military service and take all necessary precautions. We are gratified for this permission, however, as most of the people of that age are sick or disabled, their presence would make hospitals more crowded. In fact, only men of that ages are left in villages now, because of mobilisation. Their conscription would mean the evacuation of the villages and would have negative effects on the morale of the people. I therefore consider it appropriate to delay this move for the time being, after arming those able, pending their call when needed. Two artillery guns, would be sufficient for the purpose, if sent here.

Section: 1
10 (23) dated

Archive No	:	4/3641
Cabin No	:	163
Drawer No	:	2
File No	:	2820
Section No	:	69
Contents No	:	3–45, 3–46

DOCUMENT NO: 25

Office of the Acting Supreme Commander   Istanbul
of the Ottoman Army   26 April 1915
                                                (13 April 1331)

First Section
  No:
  Top Secret

To the Office of the Undersecretary
of the Ministry of National Defence

Since the Government has decided that the branches of Hinchak, Dashnak, and similar committees both in the capital and provinces will be closed down immediately; that the documents and papers at these branches will be confiscated without being destroyed; that the presidents of these committees, their leaders, active members known by the Government as well as influential and malicious Armenians will be arrested immediately; that those whose stay in their places of residence is regarded harmful will be made to stay in more suitable places and measures taken to prevent their escape; that searches for weapons will be conducted in suspicious places; that the suspect will be brought before courts martial; cooperation with administrative officials and civil servants as well as immediate response to their calls for help are hereby demanded as a priority.

                                Acting Supreme Commander
                                          Enver

This order has been conveyed to the:
First Army Command
Second Army Command
Third Army Command
Fourth Army Command
Fifth Army Command
Deputy Command of Iraq and Environs
Fourth Army Corps Command
Bosphorus Command
Dardanelles Command
Headquarters in Istanbul
Deputy 12th Army Corps Command in Mousoul
Office of the Undersecretary of the Ministry of National Defence
Army Department

Defence Department
Directorate of Judiciary

Security
240

Security Section
13 April 31 (26 April 1915)
To be preserved
16 April 31 (29 April 1915)

Archive No   :   1/131
Cabin No   :   101/149
Drawer No   :   14–4
File No   :   2287
Section No   :   32–12
Contents No   :   12–1

DOCUMENT NO: 1912 (108)

No: 5319

CODED MESSAGE FROM RESID BEY, GOVERNOR OF
DIYARBAKIR OF 14.2.331 (27 APRIL 1915).
(Received on 15 (28) dated)

Firm action has been carried against army deserters for ten days. During searches, a great number of weapons, ammunition and army uniforms were found in Armenian homes. In yesterday's searches, a great amount of explosives, 50 bombs, plenty of ammunition and weapons, state property and dynamite powder were captured. 12 members and leading figures of the villages were arrested. Up to date, over 1000 army deserters, most of them affiliated to the committee have been arrested.

Investigation and search continues.

Section   :   1–15 (28) dated
Branch   :   2–15 (28) dated
Archive No   :   4/3671
Cabin No   :   163
Drawer No   :   2
File No   :   2820
Section No   :   69
Contents No   :   3–52

DOCUMENT NO: 26
Office of the Supreme Commander   19 April 1331
of the Ottoman Army   2 May 1915
    First Section
    No: 2049 m
    To the Ministry of Interior
    Top Secret
The Armenians living around Lake Van and particularly at
certain places in the Province of Van are continually trying to stage
a revolt. I am of the opinion that this place of unrest should be
cleaned by removing these people from the region.

According to the information received from the Third Army,
the Russians drove the Muslim population, who were in wretched
condition, into our territories away from the border. Both to
achieve the goal indicated above and to retaliate to the Russian
move:

It is necessary either to drive these Armenians into Russian
territories or to disperse the Armenians and their families
throughout various places in Anatolia. I ask the selection of the
appropriate proposition and its practice. If you deem it appropriate, I prefer to drive the families of the rebels and the headquarters
of the revolt away from the borderline and to resettle the Muslim
population from abroad in the places of Armenians.

                                                        Ismet

Archive No   :   1/1
Cabin No   :   102
Drawer No   :   1
File No   :   44
Section No   :   207
Contents No   :   2–1, 2–2

DOCUMENT NO: 1916 (112)

SUBLIME PORTE
Ministry of Interior
Department for Settlement of
Tribes and Immigrants
General   :
Specific   :

REGULATION RELATED TO SETTLEMENT AND BOARD
AND LODGING AND OTHER AFFAIRS OF ARMENIANS
RELOCATED TO OTHER PLACES BECAUSE OF WAR
CONDITIONS AND EMERGENCY POLITICAL REQUIREMENTS:

Article 1 :– Arrangements for transportation of those to be transferred is the responsibility of local administrations.

Article 2 :– Armenians to be transferred are free to take all their movable properties and animals along.

Article 3 :– Protection of lives and properties of Armenians to be transferred en route their new settlements, their board and lodging and their rest is the responsibility of local administrations en route. Civil servants in all echelons are responsible for any negligence in this regard.

Article 4 :– Reaching the destinations of their new settlement, Armenians will either be settled in individual towns and villages in houses to be built, or in the villages to be established in locations designated by the Government. Due attention will be paid to establishing the villages in places which suit public health conditions, agriculture and construction.

Article 5 :– If there is no unowned and derelict land in places of settlement for establishment of villages, state owned farms and villages may be allocated for this purpose.

Article 6 :– Boundaries of villages and towns to be established anew for the settlement of Armenians will be at least 25 kilometres away from the Baghdad railroad and from other railroad links.

Article 7 :– A Registration log will be established covering very accurately in an orderly way the name, family name, age, profession, place of origin, place of settlement, together with names and ages of all members clearly indicated for all Armenians to be settled in villages and towns or in newly established villages, this log, being the basis of the population registers.

Article 8 :– Persons to be settled at the designated places, are prohibited to go to other places without permission from the Commission to which they are attached and without necessary special document from the local security force.

Article 9 :– All boarding needs of the people arriving, and the construction of houses of those who are in need, is the responsibility of the Government, such expenses to be financed from the immigrants' appropriations (funds).

Article 10 :– Arrangements of boarding and housing,

expediting the completion of these, preservation of health and welfare of the people, is the responsibility of the immigrant commissions, led by the highest local civil servant. In places where there are no immigrant commissions, these will be established anew, in accordance with the Regulation on Immigrants.

Article 11 :– District and provincial governors are authorised to assign sufficient civil servants necessary to carry out efficiently the task related to transport, board, lodging and settlement, with the concurrence of the Ministry.

Article 12 :– Each family to be resettled, will be allocated appropriate land, taking into account their previous economic condition and their present needs.

Article 13 :– Allocation and distribution of land will be handled by the commissions.

Article 14 :– Boundaries and areas of the allocated land will be indicated in a Temporary (Provisional) Receipt which will be issued to the owner, with identical information clearly registered in the special book.

Article 15 :– Those engaged in agriculture and craftsmen who are in need, will be issued an appropriate amount of operating capital, or necessary tools and instruments. Recep 333/17 May 331 (30 May 1915)

> Certified True copy.
> Seal (Department for Settlement
> of Tribes and Immigrants, Ministry of
> Interior)

Archive No	:	1/2
Cabin No	:	109
Drawer No	:	4
File No	:	361
Section No	:	1030 (1445)
Contents No	:	1

DOCUMENT NO: 1918 (114)

From Erzurum
3.5.331 (16 July 1915)
TO THE THIRD ARMY COMMAND ERZURUM

The contingent assigned to protect Armenian convoys against attacks by Kurdish gangs was attacked by Kurdish gangs from all four directions on their way through the Kop mountains on

28.4.331 (11 July 1915). The contingent, dispatched from Bayburt under the command of 2nd Lt. Salih Efendi comprised 56 enlisted men from the communications zone troops. After a two-hour armed clash, two of the gang were killed, the rest escaped. The contingent suffered no casualties and the Armenian convoy was saved, according to the information from Bayburt post.

Communications Inspector
Fuat Ziya

Section: 1/3731/4 (17) dated
File./ 4.5.31 (17 July 1915)

Archive No   : 4/3671
Cabin No   : 161
Drawer No   : 2
File No   : 2835
Section No   : 127
Contents No   : 1-11

DOCUMENT NO: 36
The coded message from Jerusalem to the Office of the Acting Supreme Commander

No: 7097   DTG

1. The Armenians to be moved away from the district of Antakya gathered at Mount Musa, north of Suveydiye, and decided to resist. A few of these Armenians took refuge on enemy warships by escaping by boat. It is possible that the cruisers "Victor Hugo" and "Henry Fastersine Louis" and three other unidentified warships took up positions in the Suveydiye region upon these Armenians' calls. Two regiments from the 41st Division and a mountain artillery team were sent against the rebels. As a result of the bombardment by warships "Victor Hugo" and "Henry Fastersine Louis" of the units and headquarters in and near Kabakli, Kabakli Village was destroyed and casualties include eight dead from military and civilians, two wounded, and 20 dead animals.

2. The detachment proceeded towards Damlat, the rebels' hide-out at midnight on August 30, 1915, but no contact took place with the rebels. This reveals that the Armenians took refuge on enemy warships at night. I am sending General Fahri to the scene of the events to punish those who permitted the escape of

Armenians and caused unnecessary casualties by not taking care
in concealing the headquarters.

3. Other Armenians in Iskenderun and Antakya are speedily
being driven away from the region. 14.9.1915 (1 Sept. 331)

Commander of the Fourth Army and
Secretary of the Navy
Cemal

Archive No	: 1–1	
Cabin No	: 10	
Drawer No	:	
File No		
:	: 13	
Section No	: 63	Second Section 2–7
Contents No	: 11	To be preserved/4–7

DOCUMENT NO: 37

Office of the Acting Supreme Commander
of the Ottoman Army
Section
No:

French Statement dated 22 September 1915

French cruisers have taken five thousand Armenian refugees,
who had been resisting since the end of July on Mount Musa, north
of Antiyuh Port and who recently ran short of ammunition and
food, and transported them to Port Said.

The Original document was given to
the Second Section on 11–7
To be preserved/ 11–7

Archive No	: 1–1
Cabin No	: 10
Drawer No	: 2
File No	: 13
Section No	: 63
Contents No	: 16

DOCUMENT NO: 41

To the Office of the Prime Minister

The people who took refuge in interior regions by escaping
from the war zone at the end of the military operations, have been

sent to new settlement places, resettled, fed, and given medical aid as well as clothes by our Directorate within the framework of the special organisation and arrangements given below in detail. The number of such refugees reached 702,900 by the end of October. Even though the people who took refuge and resettled through their own means without Government assistance are not included in the above-mentioned figure, they, too, are given financial aid when they request.

Since the beginning of 1915 when migration started, those who took refuge in cities and towns near the war zone such as Giresun, Samsun, Sivas, Elazig, Diyarbakir, and Mousoul were not kept in small squares of areas to prevent spreading contagious diseases. The refugees were also sent to places providing better sanitary conditions as well as food and resettlement possibilities. Transportation vehicles were provided for the women, children, and the sick to eliminate difficulties during transportation and care was taken to effect distribution and detachment in an orderly manner. Furthermore, health stations were set up and the refugees had vaccinations against smallpox, typhoid, typhus, and cholera.

Their nutritional needs were met during their journey and they were given hot meals in certain places. The rules and regulations concerning the administrative advice and practices to be put into effect by administrative directors and migration officials in connection with such assistance and basic protection principles have been prepared and submitted to Your Highness as Document No: 1. It has been regarded appropriate to take the utmost care in implementing these rules and regulations and to inform you briefly of the general results as follows:

The original residential places of the refugees as well as the regions selected as resettlement areas have been categorized in four groups with regard to climatic conditions, food resources, geographical resources and the general condition of transportation facilities.

"1" The refugees coming from Eastern Erzurum and the Trabzon coast have been transported to Ordu, Giresun, Unye, Samsun, Bafra, and Kastamonu via both land and sea.

"2" The refugees coming from Western and Southern Erzurum and Southern Trabzon have been transported to Ankara and neighbouring regions via the Sivas-Tokat way or to Kayseri and Nigde via Sivas-Kayseri way.

"3" The refugees coming from the southern and southeastern part of Erzurum have been transported to Elazig, Malatya and Maras via Kemah.

"4" The refugees coming from Van and Bitlis have been transported to Diyarbakir and neighbouring regions, Urfa, Gaziantep, and partially to Adana via the Diyarbakir route.

Since the transportation, resettlement, and food supplies of the refugees, the protection, feeding, and care of the widows and the orphans, and the treatment of and medical supply to the sick as well as the organization and facilities for such needs are provided and carried out in line with the local characteristics and requirements of every region, it has been regarded compulsory and appropriate to gather detailed information for every region separately.

1. The people living it [sic] Trabzon and the neighbouring coastal areas have been sent to Ordu, Giresun, and Samsun in small boats. Although this is the shortest and safest way of transportation at times of lessening enemy pressure, it could not be carried out as desired owing to the small number of boats. However, the number of people who took refuge and received government aid by this way reached twenty thousand. Even though some people have been transported by land via Karahisar and Sivas, or Niksar, Erbaa, and Amasya, the inadequate number of transportation vehicles could not bring the state of comfort and relaxation of the refugees to the desired level. Those coming from Ordu and Giresun by their own means and resettled in Terme and Carsamba, have been affected by malaria. Since further stay in this region is considered hazardous, most of them have been sent to Amasya and Merzifon and the remaining ones to those villages in the area unaffected by malaria and resettled there. Even though some of the refugees in Samsun have been affected by malaria, the distribution of quinine has lessened the effects of the disease and there have been no deaths. Some of the refugees, particularly the villagers, have been sent to Corum via Kavak, Havza, and Merzifon, and some of them to the Sinop-Kastamonu region via Bafra. The remaining group of refugees are being sent to the south within the scope of the possibilities available.

Today, the number of people who took refuge in the region is 79,100. 18,000 of these people are in Samsun, 18,000 in districts affiliated with Samsun, 4,000 are ready for transportation in Bafra, another 18,000 people are in Carsamba, 1,600 in Terme, 7,000 in districts affiliated with Terme, 18,000 in Unye and 5,500 in Fatsa.

106

Medical examination centres and food stores have been opened in Fatsa, Unye, Terme, and Carsamba for the medical treatment and feeding of the refugees going to the sub-province, by land. Refugees are given hot meals and vaccinated in these places. Furthermore, the sick are undergoing medical treatment at special hospitals opened in Samsun, Carsamba, and Unye. In the meantime, the military communications hospitals set up in Fatsa, Unye, Terme, and Carsamba are also providing assistance to the refugees in case of need. Moreover, food stores have been opened at every four hours' walking distance on the roads for meeting the nutritional needs of the group of refugees traveling from the sub-province to Sinop via Bafra or those sent to Corum via Kavak-Havza road. An orphans house and a milk centre have been opened in Samsun and all refugees are given financial aid, adults being paid 30 paras a day and the children 60 paras. Porridge, boiled and pounded wheat with meat and rice are distributed once a day to the poor and rice are distributed once a day to the poor and the physically weak refugees.

2. The refugees coming from Erzurum and its environs to Sivas are taking the Susehri and Zara-Kochisar route to Sivas. The refugees to be sent to Corum via Tokat have been sent to Tokat via Susehri-Koyulhisar-Niksar route. Since the refugees coming to Karahisar via Alucra are to be sent to Kayseri, Refahiye route and Corum.....are transported via Mesudiye-Resadiye-Niksar route. With the help of the medical examination and food supply centres as well as health institutions set up by the military, the process of transportation has taken place in an orderly and continuous way. Particularly the number of people vaccinated as a precaution against a variety of diseases reached 150,000. Even though the sub-provinces of Tokat and Amasya of the Province of Sivas are included in the resettlement regions, since the number of refugees arriving in Sivas exceeded 300,000 and their food supply and resettlement needs could not be provided to the full at the inner provinces which constitute the operations area of the Third Army, 144,964 people have been sent to the directions of Corum, Yozgat, Kayseri, Nigde, Kirsehir and Konya in various intervals and the remaining refugees were distributed houses for resettlement in the region within the boundaries of the province of Sivas. So far, a total of 8,637 houses have been distributed and 2,154 houses previously rented were also given to the refugees by abolishing rents.

The widows and orphans among the refugees have been resettled in poorhouses and vocational schools previously established in many places and extended afterwards by the provincial governments. At such places, the women and the girls are taught carpet weaving, cloth making, and sewing and the boys are trained as blacksmiths, carpenters, tailors and similar professions. Our ministry is also giving financial aid to such institutions. Milkcentres, refugee hospitals and refugee kitchens have been set up in Sivas, Yenihan, Tokat, Amasya, Merzifon, and Zile, and the distribution of hot meals and meat to the poor and infirm refugees have been taken under guarantee.

3. Those who took refuge in eastern and southern regions of Erzurum and the western region of Van are proceeding into the interior regions of the province of Elazig via Kemah or Divrigi and Kengal, or Patoguzinhan routes. Although the requisite food supply and health institutions have been hampered by the adverse physical conditions of the roads and the lack of transportation has been hampered by the adverse physical conditions of the roads and the lack of transportation vehicles.

Those who arrive in the province of Elazig are being resettled in the central sub-province, Malatya sub-province, and the districts of Adiyaman and Besni. So far approximately eighty thousand people have taken refuge in this province. Of all these refugees, 4,500 people have been resettled in the districts of Adiyaman and Besni of the central district of Malatya. Some of the remaining refugees have been sent to Diyarbakir, and the others to Maras and Gaziantep via Malatya. Regarding the food resources and accommodation facilities, this province is thought appropriate for receiving more refugees. Therefore, it has been decided to make detachments from Sivas to this province in case of need. On the road from Malatya to Elazig, beginning from Sivas, food supply centres have been set up in Deliktas, Ulus, Kangal, Alacahan, Hasan-Celebi, Hekimhan, Hasanbadrik and in the centres of Malatya-Izoli-Kadikoy and Elazig. Refugees were given hot meals in these centres. The refugees also went through medical examinations at the health centres in Kangal and Deliktas and they received medical treatment at the Kangal Communications Hospital. A hospital, orphans' house, milk centre and refugee kitchens have been set up in Harput, Elazig, and Malatya.

4. The refugees who arrived in the province of Diyarbakir from the region of Van, Bitlis, and Mus, used the Palu-Guzinhan-

Ergani or Siirt-Lice or Siirt-Silvan routes. Since the population increase in the province was over 200,000 people, it was decided to send some of the refugees to Siverek and Urfa affiliates via Siverek and the others to their pre-determined places of destination either via Mardin, Telermis, and Resulayn route or by railway with the objective of decreasing the number of people in Diyarbakir, included in the operations area of the Second Army. Following the establishment of the necessary food supply and medical centres along the Siverek road, the transportation of the refugees by railway has started. However, upon the orders given by the Second and Fourth Army commands, it is seen that the refugees to be resettled in the western region of the Taurus mountains will spend the winter in Urfa and the detachments to Islahiye by railway have been discontinued, with ceasing of transportation in Telebyaz Arab, that is Resitpinari, and detachments resumed towards Urfa. The number of people who took refuge in Diyarbakir is 16,901 at the central district and 16,162 at the district of Mardin. So far, 40,000 refugees have been sent to Urfa. The detachment is taking place in orderly groups, the refugees are fed at the food supply centres set up along the road and the groups are vaccinated to prevent contagious diseases.

A hospital and rest houses have been specially set up for the refugees in Diyarbakir. Furthermore, about 10,500 children were brought to the kindergartens set up in Diyarbakir, Mardin, Siverek and Urfa. Detachments to Gaziantep and Maras have not exceeded 15,000 people at present and it is planned to send only 10,000 people to the province of Adana. However, the necessary arrangements on this route have been made and a refugee station has been set up in Pozanti as a precaution.

All sorts of administrative means necessary for the accommodation and feeding of the refugees until they are sent to their resettlement areas have been utilized. Administrative Chiefs and Refugee Officials have been assigned with the duty of enforcing the decisions made in the Capital. A supervisor has been appointed for every region. However, as a result of the inefficiency of the branches of the Directorate General of Refugees specially set up for the accommodation of Muslim population coming from outside and of the nomadic tribes, local government officials were also assigned to deal with the problems of the refugees and the employment of officials on a daily wage basis has begun in the necessary regions.

Even though the problems of the refugees gathering together in operations area such as Samsun, Sivas-Harput, and Diyarbakir initially until they are sent to their resettlement regions have been carefully dealt with and they are given financial aid on a daily basis, their movement and nutritional needs could not be met at the desired level owing to the difficulties encountered in providing the food supply and transportation vehicles as well as the climatic conditions and the poor road conditions. Despite these difficulties, however, a food supply was found at the Communications Depots of the Second, Third and Fourth Army commands and distributed to the refugees. Furthermore, particularly the health councils of these armies provided much appreciated assistance in examining and treating the refugees.   The arrangements and facilities regarding transportation, nourishment, and accommodation are under the responsibility of the General Directorate of Refugees and Tribes of our Department and the Civil Service Control Boards have been appointed with the task of supervising the carrying out of these activities. Tackling health problems is being done through the mediation of special supervisors in harmony with the Ministry of Health. It is intended to leave the administration of the milk centres set up so far to the provincial governments. Since the extension of the scope of provincial governments is outside the authority of our Ministry, we ask the opinion of your highness about handing over the kindergartens to the Ministry of National Education afterwards.

No one should have the right to claim expertise in administering an exodus of about 800,000 people escaping from the difficulties created by the war, particularly in the face of the well-known internal situation of the country, climatic conditions and the fact that the elderly, women and children form the majority of the refugees.

However, establishment of medical examination centres along the roads, vaccination of the refugees, nourishment of the refugees at times of departure, provision of transportation vehicles to the elderly and the children, serving hot meals to those people at resting places during travelling, the partial meeting of the clothing needs of the refugees, taking care of the people disturbed by such long journeys, the meeting of the basic needs of the refugees such as accommodation and nourishment, protection of the sick, the infirm, widows, and the children at special facilities and their resettlement by providing houses and land have been conducted at

110

a satisfactory level. That is, the question of refugees is being tackled by the Prime Ministry in an admirable manner in spite of all the difficulties arising from this situation.

The total amount of money spent for the refugees reached 25 million kurus in the last year of 331. The amount of money spent by the end of October of the current year totalled 80 million kurus and approval has been given to spend at least 100 million kurus by the end of this year in order to meet only the nourishment needs of the refugees.

A schematic sketch of the institutions set up in the resettlement regions where the refugees have been and are to be transported, such as medical examination centres, hospitals, kindergartens, and workshops has been presented to the Office of the Prime Minister as document No: 2.

4 December 1916

Archive No	:	1–2
Cabin No	:	
Drawer No	:	
File No	:	361
Section No	:	1445
Contents No	:	15–22, 15–23

DOCUMENT NO: 64

Documentary No.   Signature of Copying
Section No.   Clerck
Signature of Draft Secretary
Date of drafting
Clerck No.
Section

To Acting Supreme Command
Date of Copying
Subject
Supervised (Signature)
Date of Supervision

To the Stockholm International Socialist Conference
From Beyoglu

According to reports from the Caucasian front, Armenian gangs have been murdering and inflicting cruelties on innocent people of the region. This verified information, supported by clear statements of reliable eye-witnesses, was also confirmed by General Odishelidje, Commander of the Russian Caucasian Army.

Armenians are entering every place evacuated by Russians carrying out murders, cruelties, rape and all kind of atrocities which cannot be expressed in writing, murdering all the women, children, aged people who happen to be in the street. These barbarous murders repeated every day with new methods continue and the Russian Army has been urged to intervene to terminate these atrocities. Public opinion is appalled and horrified. Newspapers are describing the happenings as shocking. We have decided to inform all our friends urgently about the situation.

Deputy of Istanbul
Socialist Salah Cimcoz
Deputy of Izmir
Socialist Nesim Mazelyah

Archive No.	:	1/2
Cabin No.	:	109
Drawer No.	:	4
File No.	:	359
Section No.	:	103 (1435)
Contents No.	:	3–20

DOCUMENT NO: 69

1.4.34 (1918)

To the 4th Army Command

Code.

Reply to code 3/34

Please be advised that from the date of the liberation of Erezurum 12 March 34 (1918) until 20 March 34, in the city of Erzurum alone the corpses of 2,127 Moslem males murdered by Armenians were found. Searches continue and your command will be further informed about any others found.

Lutfi

Archive No	:	4/3671
Cabin No	:	163
Drawer No	:	5
File No	:	2947
Section No	:	628
Contents No	:	3–4

Notes

Chapter II

1 For a general survey of the rise of Armenian nationalism see: G. Chaliand and Y. Ternon, *From Genocide to Resistance* (London: Zed Press, 1983), pp. 25–29; *Encyclopedia Hebraica* (Encyclopedia Publishing Co., 1953), pp. 971–991.

2 Chaliand and Ternon, p. 28. According to this source, three hundred thousand Armenians were killed in the events of 1895–1896. A. Corsun, *Armenian Terrorism: A Profile* (Washington, DC: Dept. of State Bulletin, August 1982), pp. 31–35.

3 Chaliand and Ternon, p. 31.

4 Documents regarding the displacement of Armenians, taken from the "Turk Tarih Kurumu Bulletini." *NATO in the 1980s,* 4–5 October 1982, the Political and Social Studies Foundation.

Many of the Turkish army's deportation directives included provisions for humanitarian conduct and for the protection of displaced Armenians. A current view maintains that a significant number of the original documents were destroyed or are still sealed in Turkey; historians and journalists have not been given access to them. It is also claimed that directives were sent by telegraph and that copies are not available. See also: Chaliand and Ternon, pp. 36–99.

5 Chaliand and Ternon, pp. 14–19.

6 L. Kuper, *Genocide* (New Haven: Yale University Press, 1981), as reported in P. Wilkinson, "Armenian Terrorism," *The World Today,* September 1983, pp. 340–350; and also a study conducted by Prof. Justin McCarthy as reported in *Wall Street Journal,* August 12, 1983.

Relatively low estimates of the number of victims usually correlated to lower assessments of the total Armenian population in Turkey, especially in the eastern provinces, on the eve of World War I. See also: R. W. Howe, "Armenian Saga," *Washington Times,* August 1–3, 1983.

7 With regard to the trial of the heads of the Committee of Union and Progress, see: "Extracts from the Memoirs of American Ambassador Henry Morgenthau," in Chaliand and Ternon, pp. 74–97.

8 For a summary of the period of combat and the relevant political processes in Turkey, 1918–1923, see: Chaliand and Ternon, pp. 109–119.

9 *Ibid; Encyclopedia Hebraica,* pp. 971–991.

10 Chaliand and Ternon, p. 118.

11 *Ibid;* R.W. Howe, "Armenian Saga," August 3, 1983.

12 "The Armenian issue in nine questions and answers," *On the Armenian Question,* Publication No. 3 (Ankara: Foreign Policy Institute, June 1982), p. 34; R.W. Howe, "Armenian Saga," August 3, 1983.

13 See below, Chapter 8, "Turkey's Attitude toward Armenian Terrorism."

14 *Wall Street Journal,* August 16, 1983.

Chapter III

15 *Executive Risk Assessment* (prepared by Risks International, Inc., Alexandria, Virginia), August 1983, p. 19.

16 *Al–Watan al–Arabi* (Lebanon), March 3, 1983.

17   For a characteristic interpretation of Asala's objectives along these lines, see *Wall Street Journal,* February 1, 1982.

18   A. Corsun, *Armenian Terrorism.*

19   ASALA's political platform, in *Al–Nashara* (Cyprus), October 31, 1983.

20   *Ibid.*

21   M.M. Gunter, "The Armenian Terrorist Campaign Against Turkey," *Orbis,* Summer 1983, pp. 447–477.

22   A. Corsun, *Armenian Terrorism.*

23   *Executive Risk Assessment,* December 1982, p. 16.

24   *Wall Street Journal,* August 16, 1983.

25   *Ha'aretz* (Israel), July 18, 1983; *AP,* July 20, 1983; *International Herald Tribune,* July 21, 1983.

26   *Guardian,* September 6, 1983.

27   *Al–Watan al–Arabi,* August 5, 1983.

28   *Guardian,* September 6, 1983.

Chapter IV

29   *Al Hamishmar* (Israel), August 3, 1983.

30   *Ma'ariv* (Israel), March 22, 1983.

31   *Al–Watan al–Arabi,* March 17, 1983.

32   *Defense and Foreign Affairs Weekly,* IX, nos. 33, 49 (August 22–28, 1983).

33   *Al Hamishmar,* July 22, 1983; *Wall Street Journal,* August 16, 1983.

34   *Executive Risk Assessment,* December 1982, p. 16.

35   *Le Monde,* July 19, 1983.

36   *Tercuman* (Turkey), May 24, 1983, in *Turkish Diplomatic Pulse.*

37   *Ibid.*

38   AP (Beirut), August 2, 1982; *Jerusalem Post* (Israel), August 6, 1982.

39   *Washington Post,* July 19, 1983.

40   *Ma'ariv,* July 19, 1983; *Newsweek,* August 1, 1983; *Economist Foreign Report,* no. 1783 (July 21, 1983).

41   *Al–Watan al–Arabi,* March 17, 1983.

42   Ibid., August 5, 1983.

43   *Executive Risk Assessment,* August 1982, p. 19.

44   *Al–Majalla* (Saudi Arabia), August 21, 1983.

45   *Defense and Foreign Affairs Weekly,* IX, nos. 35, 51 (September 5–11, 1983).

46   *Guardian,* September 6, 1983.

47   *Washington Post,* May 7, 1984.

48   *Armenian Reporter,* May 17, 1979.

49   A. Corsun, *Armenian Terrorism;* UPI, August 8, 1983 (based on Turkish sources).

50   *Milliyet* (Turkey), May 6, 1983; *Hurriyet* (Turkey), May 9, 1983.

51   *Executive Risk Assessment,* December 1982, p. 16.

52   *Wall Street Journal,* August 16, 1983.

Chapter V

53   *Al–Watan al–Arabi,* March 17, 1983.

54   *Ma'ariv,* March 22, 1982.

55 Anatolia agency in English, April 6, 1981, in *BBC Summary of World Broadcasts,* HE/6695/C/1, April 9, 1981.

56 *Executive Risk Assessment,* May 1981, p. 17; *Ma'ariv,* June 23, 1980, and September 5, 1982.

57 *Ma'ariv,* October 5, 1981.

58 *Tercuman,* August 9, 1982.

59 C. Sterling, *The Terrorist Network* (New York: Holt, Rinehart & Winston, 1981); *Los Angeles Times,* January 25, 1981.

60 *Tercuman,* June 20, 1981.

61 *International Herald Tribune,* January 25, 1981.

62 *Economist Foreign Report,* no. 1740 (August 19, 1982); *Turkish Digest.* August 26, 1982. See below, ch. 5.

63 *Jerusalem Post,* August 26, 1982.

64 *Al Hamishmar,* August 3, 1982.

65 *Ma'ariv,* November 15, 1982; *International Herald Tribune,* January 24, 1982; *Executive Risk Assessment,* February 1982, p. 17.

66 *Le Point,* November 23, 1980.

67 *Turkish Diplomatic Pulse* (Turkey), June 7, 1982.

68 *Yediot Aharonot* (Israel), May 19, 1983.

69 *Ma'ariv,* November 20, 1980.

70 *Milliyet,* August 21, 1982.

71 *Executive Risk Assessment,* August 1982, p. 19.

72 *Gunes* (Turkey), August 9, 1982.

73 *Economist Foreign Report,* no. 1740 (August 19, 1982).

74 *Economist Foreign Report,* no. 1783 (July 21, 1983); *Ma'ariv,* July 17, 1983; *Davar* (Israel), July 24, 1983.

75 *New York Times,* September 27, 1981.

76 *Washington Post,* September 9, 1981.

77 *Al–Watan al–Arabi,* 5, 1983; Beirut Voice of Lebanon in Arabic, September 26, 1981, in *Daily Report,* Middle East and Africa. Foreign Broadcast and Information Service, vol. 5, no. 187 (September 28, 1981).

78 *Gunes,* July 26, 1982.

79 *Turkish Diplomatic Pulse,* March 31, 1981.

80 *Hurriyet,* August 25, 1982.

81 *Executive Risk Assessment,* December 1982, p. 16.

82 *Gunaydin* (Turkey), July 2, 1982.

83 *Newsweek,* August 1, 1981.

84 *Economist Foreign Report,* no. 1788 (August 25, 1983).

85 *Ibid.*

86 *AP* (Beirut), November 10, 1980.

87 *The (Turkish) Press Digest,* July 12, 1982.

88 *Hurriyet,* December 31, 1981.

89 *Hurriyet,* March 9, 1981.

90 *Tercuman,* April 4, 1981.

91 *Executive Risk Assessment,* August 1982, p.19.

92 *Executive Risk Assessment,* March 1980, p. 14.

93 *Al–Nashara,* October 31, 1983.

94 *Daily Telegraph,* January 5, 1981.

95 *Ibid; Tercuman,* August 9, 1983.

96 *Economist Foreign Report,* No. 1740 (August 19, 1982).

97 Voice of Lebanese Armenians in Armenia (clandestine), February 2, 1983, in *Daily Report,* Middle East and Africa. Foreign Broadcast Information Service, vol. 5, no. 032 (February 17, 1982). See also ASALA's political platform in *Al–Nashara,* October 31, 1983.

98 *Economist Foreign Report,* no. 1788 (August 25, 1983).

99 *Le Figaro,* September 25, 1981.

100 *Al Hamishmar,* April 22, 1982.

101 *Ibid.,* April 22, 1982.

102 *Executive Risk Assessment,* May 1983, p. 1; *Economist Foreign Report,* no. 1788 (August 25, 1983); *Wall Street Journal,* September 19, 1983.

103 *Al–Watan al–Arabi,* March 17, 1983.

104 *Wall Street Journal,* September 19, 1983.

105 *Al Hamishmar,* July 22, 1983.

106 *Gunes,* August 8, 1982; *Tercuman,* August 8, 1982.

107 *Ma'ariv,* October 28, 1983.

108 *Executive Risk Assessment,* May 1983, p. 1; *Economist Foreign Report,* no. 1783 (July 21, 1983).

109 *Defense and Foreign Affairs Weekly,* IX, nos. 33, 49 (August 22–28, 1983); IX, nos. 39, 55 (October 10–16, 1983).

110 *Al–Nashara,* October 31, 1983.

111 *Economist Foreign Report,* no. 1783 (July 21, 1983).

112 *Executive Risk Assessment,* September 1982, p. 34.

113 *Ibid.,* September 1982.

114 *Ibid.,* May 1983, p. 1.

115 *Ibid.*

116 *Gunaydin,* April 12, 1981.

117 *Executive Risk Assessment,* May 1983, p. 1.

Chapter VI

118 *The Economist,* August 14, 1982; *Newspot — Turkish Digest* (Ankara), September 10, 1982.

119 *Washington Post,* July 19, 1983.

120 *The Economist,* July 23, 1983.

121 *Ibid.*

122 *Ibid.*

123 *Al–Watan al–Arabi,* August 5, 1983.

Chapter VII

124 *Tercuman,* June 3, 1983.

125 *Executive Risk Assessment,* February 1982, p. 17.

126 *Economist Foreign Report,* no. 1783 (July 21, 1983).

127 *Washington Post,* May 4, 1984.

128 "Terrorism in France," *Conflict Studies,* no. 144 (1983).

129 *International Herald Tribune,* February 1, 1984; *Ha'aretz,* February 2, 1984.

130 *Economist Foreign Report,* no. 1783 (July 21, 1983); *Ha'aretz,* October 10, 1983.

131 *Tercuman,* April 4, 1983.

132 *International Herald Tribune,* July 28, 1982.

133 *Executive Risk Assessment,* September 1982, p. 34.

134 *AP,* July 20, 1983; *International Herald Tribune,* July 25, 1983.

135 Chaliand and Ternon, p. 4.

136 *The Economist,* July 23, 1983.

Chapter VIII

137 "The Armenian issue in nine questions and answers."

138 Chaliand and Ternon, pp. 3–4. In recent years Turkey's diplomatic victories in international bodies such as the UN have usually been made possible by concessions to the Islamic bloc and, through it, to the nonaligned bloc.

139 "The Armenian issue in nine questions and answers."

140 *Ma'ariv,* October 11, 1983.

141 *Executive Risk Assessment,* December 1982, p. 16.

142 *Al–Majalla,* June 25, 1983.

143 *Defense and Foreign Affairs Weekly,* IX, no. 35, 51 (September 5–11, 1983); IX, nos. 35, 55 (October 10–16, 1983).

Chapter IX

144 ASALA claimed responsibility for two attacks on El Al offices in Rome: on December 9, 1979, and on February 9, 1980. It has not acted against Israeli or Jewish targets since then. Some militant groups in the Armenian nationalist movement evidently have an ambivalent attitude toward Zionism and Israel. Though ASALA has attacked Zionism verbally, this is probably only lip service to Palestinian organizations with whom it has close relations. This may explain the declaration of an unidentified ASALA commander, as reported in the Cyprus newspaper *Al–Nashara* on October 31, 1983: "We view Zionist institutions as enemy targets, but at the moment they are not included among our main targets. We leave responsibility for attacks on them to the Palestinian Revolution whose men we support in their struggle."

Similarly, the link between Zionism and imperialism as enemies of the nationalist struggle of many peoples is a formula accepted among organizations and states with leftist ideologies. But such rhetoric does not necessarily imply an intent to take direct action. Even when ASALA attacked Israeli targets, this was done within the context of concentrated attacks on western travel bureaux — which were chosen for their commercial ties to Turkey, rather than because they represented "imperialist" states.

At the same time, any step Israel takes against ASALA (for example, arresting one of its members), would presumably lead to offensive action by the organization. This has been ASALA's policy on similar occasions in the past when European countries were involved.

145 *The Economist,* July 23, 1983.

Appendix 1

146 *Executive Risk Assessment,* May 1983, p. 1.

147 Bonnie Cordes, et al., "Armenian Terrorism," *Trends in International Terrorism 1982 and 1983* (Santa Monica: Rand, August 1984), pp. 19–25.

148 *Tercuman,* July 14, 1983.

JCSS Publications

JCSS publications present the findings and assessments of the Center's research staff. Each paper represents the work of a single investigator or a team. Such teams may also include research fellows who are not members of the Center's staff. Views expressed in the Center's publications are those of the authors and do not necessarily reflect the views of the Center, its trustees, officers, or other staff members or the organizations and individuals that support its research. Thus the publication of a work by JCSS signifies that it is deemed worthy of public consideration but does not imply endorsement of conclusions or recommendations.

Editor
Aharon Yariv

Executive Editor
Joseph Alpher

Editorial Board

Mordechai Abir
Yehezkel Dror
Saul Friedlander
Shlomo Gazit
Mordechai Gur
Yehoshafat Harkabi
Walter Laqueur

Yuval Ne'eman
Yitzhak Rabin
Aryeh Shalev
Israel Tal
Saadia Touval
David Vital

The Jaffee Center for Strategic Studies – Recent Publications in English